on life and architecture

DAVID MACKAY

The object of this little book is to help us all to understand the role of architecture
in forming the built environment within which we live our daily lives. Its effect on our health,
wellbeing and happiness should not be underestimated. The responsibility is ours.

David Mackay Hon FRIAS

December 2013

First Published 2013 by

The Royal Incorporation of Architects in Scotland, Edinburgh

Text: David Mackay

Editor: Neil Baxter

Design: Jon Jardine (mail@jonjardine.com)

ISBN: 978-1-873190-68-5

A catalogue record for this book is available from the British Library.

Work table in our office (sketchbook), Plaça Reial, Barcelona, Catalonia (2003)

Printed and bound in Great Britain by Bell & Bain Ltd, Glasgow

ACKNOWLEDGEMENTS

Many people have assisted me with this book. It would never have seen the light of day without their help. In the first place, Pere Tió, editor of La Mansarda Editorial, who commissioned the book to be published in Catalan. For three months he battled with me over the proposed structure while we were drinking gin and tonic, sitting outside the Velòdrom bar in Barcelona's Calle Muntaner.

While the financial crisis delayed the Catalan publication, the Royal Incorporation of Architects in Scotland stepped in to publish it as a supplement to the *RIAS Quarterly*. I have a longstanding relationship with the Royal Incorporation, an excellent organisation which truly supports its members while being thoroughly international in its outlook. Particular thanks to Iain Connelly, RIAS President, and the Secretary and Treasurer, Neil Baxter, who also kindly spent five days exhaustively correcting the text into current English for this author in voluntary exile in Barcelona and introduced the idea of illustrating the book with my own sketches and drawings. He also masterminded the production of this edition.

I must also thank my eldest son, John, director of the Official School of Languages in Granollers, Barcelona, who together with two friends, Maria Luchetti and Graciela Estavan, three non-architects, read the text to smooth out architectural language for the general reader.

Maria Bohigas kindly helped me to find and select many of the sketches. Also thanks to the staff who eased my task searching through a thousand files at the Historic Archive at the College of Architects of Catalonia who now hold the MBM Architects archive. The book would never have existed without the help of Anna Górriz, my personal assistant, who patiently typed out and corrected every draft until this final, hopefully presentable version.

Neil Baxter's personal assistant, Carol-Ann Hildersley, also assisted immensely by correcting and re-correcting the edited drafts. Jon Jardine, the brilliant Scottish graphic designer who resides in Berlin, once again applied his magic touch and added much beauty to the publication. Penultimate thoughts of profound gratitude go to the partners and colleagues (all listed within the book's covers) who have been fellow travellers on this architectural journey. However, it is to my wife Roser Jarque and the family we built together that I once again pledge my final thoughts of deepest and eternal gratitude.

David Mackay Hon FRIAS
MBM Arquitectes

Born of an Irish father and an English mother in Eastbourne, Sussex on Christmas Day 1933 and trained in England, David Mackay has lived and worked in Barcelona for nearly 60 years. The practice, founded by his partners Oriol Bohigas and Josep Martorell, MBM Arquitectes, has evolved as one of the pre-eminent architectural practices in Europe. Their work has helped shape many cities and fundamentally influenced the evolution of European architecture and city planning.

Martorell, Bohigas and Mackay's work is characterised by its simplicity of form and human scale. They create urban spaces which are welcoming to their inhabitants and add to the vibrancy of cities. David Mackay's high-profile projects have included the urban design of the Barcelona Olympic Village in 1992 and the Design Museum in Barcelona.

David writes and lectures widely and has been guest professor at Washington University, Saint Louis and Wisconsin University, Milwaukee. In 2004, he was awarded an Honorary Doctorate by the University of Plymouth. He is also an Honorary Member of the Bund Deutscher Architekten, Honorary Fellow of the Royal Institute of the Architects of Ireland and a loyal and supportive friend and Honorary Fellow of the RIAS.

PREFACE

The renowned international architect David Mackay Hon FRIAS has a special relationship with Scotland and in particular with the Royal Incorporation of Architects in Scotland. He has contributed his wisdom to several RIAS Annual Conventions, judged four major Scottish competitions, lectured to Scottish architecture students and, in 2009, his illustrated autobiography *A Life in Cities* was published by the Royal Incorporation with funding from the Glasgow Institute of Architects.

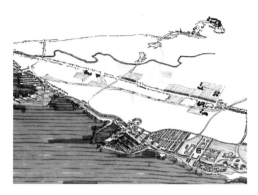

Waterfront urban design, Edinburgh, Scotland (1995)

The preface to *A Life in Cities* mentions the popular misconception that David Mackay is a Scot. He has even been introduced as such before a large international audience in his adoptive city, Barcelona. To his credit, David has never contradicted the notion that he had his origins in Scotland. In one sense, he does, David often fondly describes his first experience of a major city, as a war time émigré visitor to Glasgow, as a defining moment, whenever he reflects on his long career, dedicated to shaping cities, through architecture and masterplanning.

This essay, written and published on the eve of David Mackay's 80th Birthday, is the culmination of a lifetime's exploration of the effects of architecture on the human condition. David is an extraordinarily erudite, extremely well-read and thoroughly decent man. His personal pursuit has always been an architecture which fundamentally enhances the human condition. His own building projects, often understated, always contextual and invariably transformative of the lives lived in and around them, testify to his skill, sensitivity and care.

This essay brings together David's lifelong polymathic reading, the thinking expressed through his own work, his observations of the work of others and his studies and experience of the human condition. It contains lessons for his fellow architects and for the politicians, civil servants and clients who influence the evolution of our human habitations. It is a gift, written, with characteristic generosity, as an 80th birthday present from one of Europe's most gentle and thoughtful architects, in the hope of making a difference.

Iain Connelly, President
The Royal Incorporation of Architects in Scotland
December 2013

Temporary residence for families with children with cancer,
Vall d'Hebrón neighbourhood, Barcelona, Catalonia (2006)

CONTENTS

A SHORT INTRODUCTION

so what is architecture?

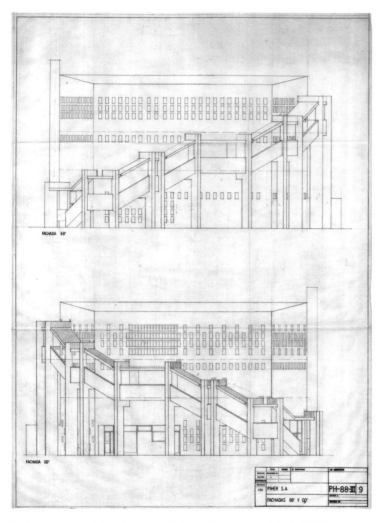

Factory canteen and changing rooms, Badalona, Barcelona, Catalonia (1962)

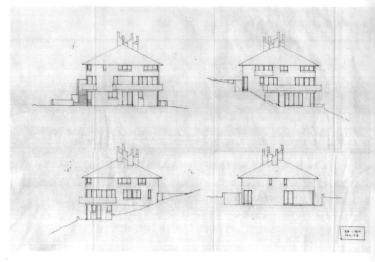

House at 1,500m altitude, Tredòs. Vall d'Aràn, Catalonia (1966)

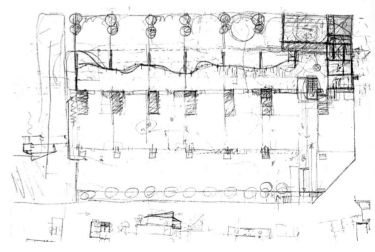

Infant School, Ciutadella, Minorca, Balearic Islands (1975)

So What is Architecture?

From my window I can see the yellow dome of the *Parliament of Catalonia*. And now we are in the lightness of spring, the tracery of trees allows me to locate it. Soon the foliage will draw a curtain of liquid green between this relatively new symbol of democracy and the red tiled roof of the *University Pompeu Fabra*. The *University*, like the *Parliament building*, replaces former occupation by a military authority.

Beyond the yellow dome is the delicate profile of the prickly spire of the popular *Castle of the Three Dragons*. Used as a restaurant during the International exhibition of 1888, in the Ciutadella Park, the *Castle* still emerges from the tree-line, as a reminder of the opening gambit in Barcelona's bid to recover its proper place in the family of European cities. Moving my eyes to the right, another more solemn spire, of regal intentions, announces the *Palace of Justice*.

The late afternoon light, accompanied by the silent embrace of a sea mist, dilutes the intrusion of the scatter of stub ends of crudely finished taller slabs into the city skyline's silhouette. They are the sinister companions of a more careful architecture.

Windows, up to the sixth or seventh floor, allow us to connect with the street, to its moments of bustle and moments of silence. From the privacy of our rooms, we can observe the life of the neighbourhood, comfortably familiar, extending our sense of sharing a space with others we know, mixed with the flow of strangers passing by.

Looking out of a window implies a consideration of what you see. This is the first move to register, perhaps subconsciously, in the mind and memory, forms and elements of architecture, or what some refer to as our built environment.

Naturally we look out of the window to see what is going on outside: a car or bicycle going by, children coming back from school, neighbours who have stopped to chat, a cat emerging from under a parked car. We observe a fleeting moment of activity, which includes the state of the weather, within a space delineated by the window frame itself and by the buildings in the street, or square, which in turn contribute to the architectural sequence of the larger settlement.

Shakespeare must have been looking out of a window, real or metaphorical, when he observed, "All the world's a stage, and all the men and women merely players". Architecture is that stage, a stage for people at home, work, leisure, and for forming urban settlements and public spaces that connect.

So what is architecture?

Let's begin by quoting a random selection of opinions. In 1883, the French architectural historian, Charles Chipiez, together with the architect Hellenist Georges Perrot, wrote that, "No satisfactory definition has ever been given of the word architecture, and yet when we use it everyone knows what we mean".

This seems an intelligent approach to our subject. The quotation embraces many variables that change with every generation, situation and culture and leaves it open as a question, because "everyone knows what we mean". This last phrase embraces "everyone". Architecture is around all of us, everywhere. It affects the way we live, in either a positive or negative way, depending on how we respond to the spaces we occupy, in different times and places.

The architect and academic, W.R. Lethaby, is considered a precursor of the Modern Movement. Concerned with the social values of architecture in 1891 he wrote, "Architecture is the art of building and of disposing buildings". This is probably the most precise definition yet. Lethaby combines creative intuition and history embodied in the word "art". He is concerned not only with the form of buildings but also adds the concept of urban design in his allusion to the relationship between buildings and their setting, when he adds "and of disposing buildings". His view of architecture takes us into the social, or public, responsibility of architecture, one of the fundamental pillars of the Modern Movement in architecture.

The architectural historian Geoffrey Scott is known mainly for his one book on Renaissance architecture, *The Architecture of Humanism*, considered by many to be a masterpiece. Scott defines the principal characteristic of architecture as the void rather than the solid. In 1914 he claimed, "Architecture alone of the Arts can give space its full value. It can surround us with a void of three dimensions and whatever delight may be derived from that is the gift of architecture alone... architecture deals with space directly; it uses space as a material and sets us in the midst".

Sculpture, a three dimensional art, also plays with space, setting itself in the midst, while the observer moves around. Occasionally with larger works the viewer dwells within. In the latter situation the sculptor trespasses into architecture. Vice-versa, some architects today trespass into urban space, using the exterior form of their buildings as giant sculptures. Lethaby would surely condemn such practice as socially and publicly irresponsible if it became a mere style, independent of its setting.

The Italian architectural historian and academic, Bruno Zevi was generally considered a maverick amongst classicists for his libertarian defence of architecture as rupture and fragmentation, and his advocacy of asymmetry and dissonance, a feature of modernity. Curiously, at the same time he follows Geoffrey Scott in pin-pointing that the void should be the protagonist of architecture. Writing in 1957 he goes on to point out that "Architecture is not art alone, it is not merely a reflection of concepts of life or a portrait of systems of living. Architecture is environment, the stage on which our lives unfold".

So as we gaze out of the window, we are observing life unfolding on a stage, not necessarily consciously considering that it is architecture which makes our urban environment. The question is now the reverse of the French historians, Chipez and Perrot. Few observers out of windows realise that they are immersed every day within architecture that, good or bad, is a man-made creation. Therefore an artificial, man-made, world surrounds the spaces on both sides of the window.

This rather broad selection of approaches helps us define what architecture is, or what it's all about and how we cannot ignore it. Perhaps we can relate its structure to that of chess. There are many pieces, each have their particular moves. At the same time, they must work together. The battle, representing the opposing array of pieces in the struggle, is perhaps analogous to the process of creating architecture. By understanding the problems, and the various roles that must be combined to reach the final objective, one can appreciate the solution better, be it a building, a group of buildings, or a city. Whether you like or dislike the architecture is another question.

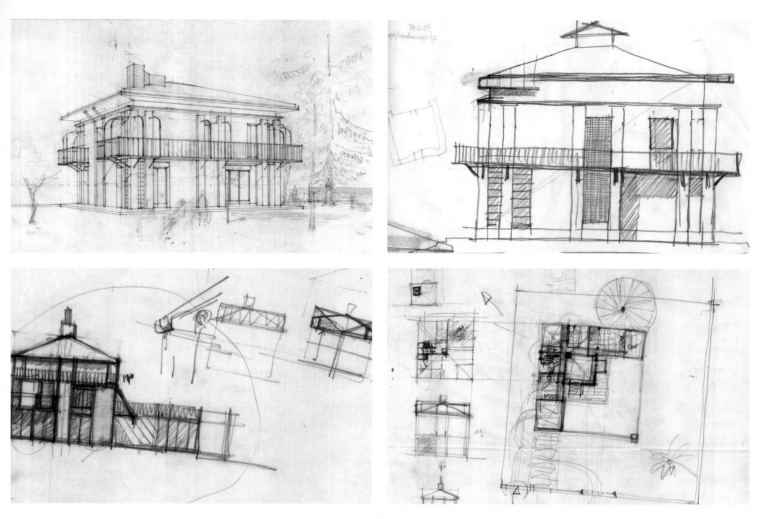

House (after Schinkel, Berlin), La Garriga, Barcelona, Catalonia (1975)

It is curious to consider this relationship of architecture to chess, a relationship that I personally discovered, reflecting on my own career, after reading a commentary by the Italian architect Renzo Piano. Today, in the process of designing architecture, it is necessary to establish a dialogue between the pencil in the hand and the computer.

The human brain contains more resources than any computer, the accumulation of experience with the short circuit of intuition to help find solutions. The architect's pencil traces ideas quicker than the computer, imagination links unusual sources with the added advantage of improvisation. This can be "corrected" later with the precision of computer software.

In practice the computer drawing, though exact and allowing several people to work from a common base, demands,

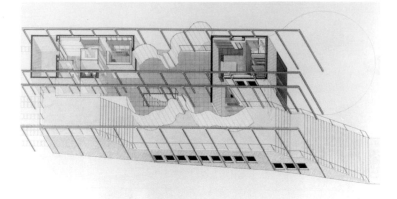

House, Granollers, Barcelona, Catalonia (1977)

107

Romanesque Church (sketchbook), Taüll. Vall de Boi, Catalonia (1978)

too soon, the exact measurement before a line can be drawn. It lacks the freedom of the pencil line. As somebody remarked, today's projects need hardware, software and fleshware (the operator) to produce the required result.

At this moment I began to reflect on the human structure of "fleshware", the capacity of the imagination to recall simultaneously all the appropriate factors to be transmitted, through the point of the pencil on paper, the intuitive origins of an architectural design. This is appropriately called a "sketch". If we exchange the references to architecture for chess we can sense a close relationship of the thought process between the two.

There is, of course, a similar argument for the relationship between chess and football. Following the Barça of Pep Guardiola, I was fascinated how the team moved with the choreography of a ballet, according to the precise strategy of a chess game, an expression of a team working at its highest level.

The Russian chess master and critic, E.A. Znosko-Borovsky wrote that the material basis of the game is a combination of space, time and force. In order to succeed one had to understand the value of the idea of space. Time is related to how you move through space. If you move incorrectly you loose the time necessary to assemble a strategic plan. However that is not always true because some moves are voluntary, others are forced to make you loose time. He also adds that, although moves are equal in point of time, it is important that they should be made at the right moment.

The analogy with architecture is clear. You begin by considering space, but the structural order of the strategic occupation or delineation of that space (assembling the programme, site conditions, materials, costs, clients, ideas, planning restrictions, light, views, entrances, roof, structure, etc.) all impinge upon the emerging vision of the final result in the mind of the architect. The work of the architect is to achieve the final cultural result. The work of the engineer is confined to the joy of the process itself.

To space and time the Russian chess master adds the crucial word "force". The importance of this to chess is the capacity of each piece to combine space and time, realising that each piece has a different capacity, according to its relative importance in different games. In architecture each period of time can determine the architect's choice of which piece is the most important, say current cultural attitudes, technological advances, climate, economy, social concern, etc., not forgetting the role of the client.

Architecture is an art, but without a client there can be no architecture. There is no chess game if there is only one player. Most clients are of course frustrated architects. So the strategy of the architect must be one of gentle persuasion. The difficulty arises when the client is an administration, public or private, without the cultural leadership that can assume the role of frustrated architect client that everybody experiences at some time or other, be it re-positioning furniture or the thrill of arranging the elements within a dream home, office or palace.

The quality of urban design and public facilities, like schools, can be lost when there is a cultural void within a brief that is only concerned with legal issues and costs. Understanding how architecture is born can help us to read the built environment. We can read it through words, a more academic discipline or we can read the image that we observe, a more aesthetic, perhaps even a more visceral approach. Both contribute to our knowledge and understanding, enhancing our critical faculties and pleasure in our environment.

So, sticking with the analogy of architecture with chess, we can now embark on the "opening gambit", to consider the different pieces, or questions involved, and how do they contribute to distinguishing a building, or a group of buildings, or a part of the city as "architecture".

We have started with the view from a window. Perhaps we can examine the role of the window in architecture, and in European culture as a whole. This will be our first topic towards an understanding of architecture: the enclosing division between the inside and outside and the connect and disconnect between the two.

The old city (sketchbook), Jeddah, Saudi-Arabia (1979)

15

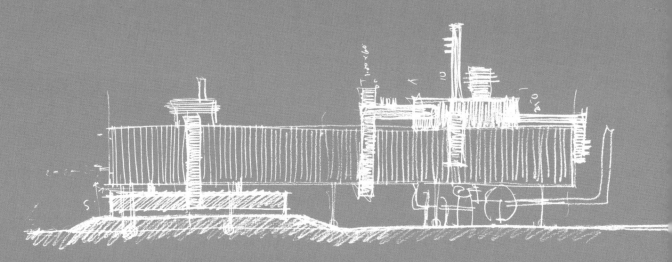
Factory for semiconductors, Granollers, Barcelona, Catalonia (1972)

all the world's
a stage

 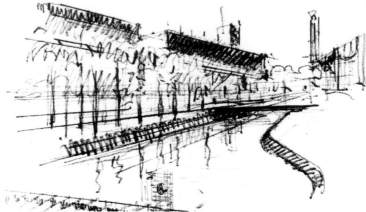

Social housing, Barceloneta neighbourhood, Barcelona, Catalonia (1979)

Inside or Outside? That is the Question

Oriental art communicates the unlimited space through the ever rolling scroll and sliding screens. Western culture has preferred the limitations of the frame and the window to tempt the imagination to the space beyond the given view.

Let me explain. Wherever we go we find framed pictures hanging on a wall or placed on a shelf. Whatever the medium, these images stimulate the mind to wander around memories and dreams. They become part of our short life, sharing the creative observation with the past and present. Many of us go to exhibitions, but all of us look out, or look in, through the window frames of the buildings we inhabit or pass by. Apart from visually trespassing through the window frame, either from the inside to the outside, or vice-versa, the window acts as a filter for borrowed light and captured air.

There are many ways to filter light and air. However rather than straying into a lengthy study of the various types of windows we can skim over some of the most obvious. Windows range from an open vertical slit in the wall, with perhaps a wooden shutter, to the circular Roman eye known as an oculus, or from translucent alabaster, to the use of glass and its supporting lead or stone sub-frames. Then there are the various ways of opening windows, including the normal casement, opening inwards or outwards, sash windows sliding up and down, or horizontal sliding windows. These examples just show us how we are involved every day with windows. They form a fundamental part of the way we live, though we do not always realise it.

In English, the word window itself comes from the Norse "vindauga". "Vind" means wind, and "auga" means eye, just like the Roman "oculus". A window is the eye that enables us to see, but also allows ventilation or protection from the wind. The Spanish "ventana" also derives from the Norse. The Catalan "finestra" derives from the Latin or Etruscan source, like fenêtre in French and fenster in German, which refers to a window with glass. In Mediterranean countries it is possible that, early on, light only came from the Patio, and cross ventilation came from the wooden shutters in the outside wall, suggesting this arrangement was for privacy or security.

Today the technology of mechanical engineering has robbed architecture of its windows, and its human relationship. Entirely glazed walls, apart from sealing the interior from "natural" winds, eliminate the culture of the framed focused view, in exchange for all over views, giving a sense of power to the viewer. This uncomfortably reminds one of the Devil's temptation of Christ, or Hitler's constant desire to look down to the world below from his retreat near Berchtesgaden, or for that matter, the financial gods in their urban glass towers.

I remember once reading an observation by a school teacher. He explained that if he saw a child in his class distractedly looking out of the window, he wouldn't call the child's attention back to the lesson. In his view the child was observing life itself outside –perhaps a butterfly, a falling leaf, a passing cloud or the threat of rain, all of which was as important as the lesson.

The window is an eye to knowledge outside, like the lesson inside. It is odd that you cannot have a window without a wall, but you can have a wall without a window, like those that divide a country, like the *Berlin Wall*, or surround it, like Israel, the first to keep their East German citizens in, and the second to keep the Palestinians out.

A wall is a limit, usually to protect private property, a challenge for a child to climb over and pluck apples from the trees next door. The wall determines physical limits. Either in

a friendly way, to protect an interior from the weather, or the noise from neighbours, or when used structurally, to support the building.

When it is necessary to include windows within the enveloping wall of a house, or any other building, the architect has to consider the needs arising from the use and location of the interior spaces with the composition of the façade as seen from the outside. This latter consideration depends on the client and architect's attitude towards the city and its streets. Every building forms part of the city, so there are certain obligations towards fellow citizens and the legacy from the past.

For an architect the composition of the openings in the façade presents an immense challenge to his ability to design. Normally every room needs one or more windows, but some rooms require different treatment from others, depending on the importance of use and which floor it is on. However, at the same time, the design of the window must relate to its

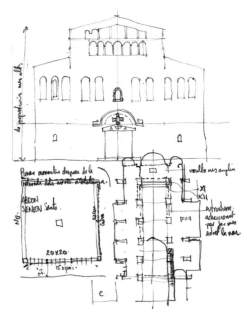

Romanesque Monastery (sketchbook), Roussillon, France (1980)

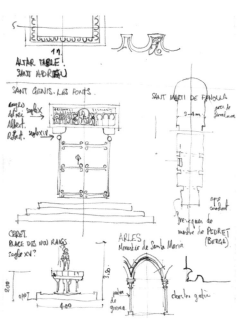

Romanesque fragments (sketchbook), Provence, France (1980)

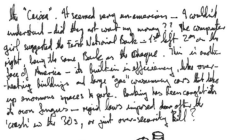

Burger with Cheshire cheese (sketchbook), Saint Louis, USA (1981)

19

orientation, to the different climatic conditions relating to the sun, time of the day, and in some cases, the importance of the view.

With the withdrawal from the stress of the city, first by the privileged, to relaxed villas, palaces or country houses, in the fifteenth century, the enclosing walls began to be pierced to delineate an outside room or loggia. At first the move to the country was a desire for seclusion, protected by the space of the landscape. Appreciation of the value of the walled garden, extending the territory of the owners, grew over time.

These country estates provided excellent opportunities for entertaining guests. This facilitated the exchange of information, valuable in the pursuit of influence in the powerful circles of merchants and the royal courts. This is still true today, six centuries later.

The variety of approaches to dealing with the spaces on the inside and outside of the enclosing wall increased as social habits changed. The variety of solutions becoming ever wider. We may be very familiar with many of these solutions to link the inside space with the exterior. Just because we take them for granted we may not fully realise the qualities they give to make a room more attractive.

Let's begin with the balcony.

Its first appearance was to allow a public address to call citizens to pray in the Islamic tradition, or for a political leader to address his subjects. The frequent appearance of the British Royal family on the *Buckingham Palace* central balcony for state occasions is a well-known example, shown on the BBC to the world. A similar example can be observed in Barcelona when the President of the Generalitat appears after winning an election, also on a central balcony.

In domestic architecture the balcony-window allows the perception of being able to leave the confinement of a room.

On an upper floor an ordinary window creates the feeling of being in a box overlooking the city. On the other hand, the natural light effect of a balcony is different, allowing the sunlight to dance in, moving across the floor as time slips by, eliminating the box effect.

The difference between a balcony and a projecting terrace from an upper floor in an urban context, is that the latter loses the intimacy of the balcony. By observation, the terrace seems to be of little use, except for drying the laundry. At the moment of buying the flat the terrace is sold on the dream of a hanging garden. These terraces often become enclosed glazed galleries, claiming a useful space and bringing it indoors.

Now let's look at the thickness of the wall itself.

When walls were thick, and generally of stone, while ensuring structural safety and defence, they also retained the summer heat for the cold winters, or the coolness of the winter for the warm summers. Even today if you enter, say a Cistercian monastery, you notice the difference in the temperature. Small windows in thick walls also play their part in sustaining the required temperature, often accompanied by splayed jambs, or embrasure, to reflect the light, correcting the loss from the reduced dimensions of the window itself.

Splayed jambs within the thickness of the wall in domestic rooms, incorporated stone benches on either side for conversation, and for keeping an eye glancing out of the window. We are all familiar with the children's romantic tales of the princess waiting for her prince, confined within the castle tower, sitting by the window. Even today Catalan farmhouses have twin stone benches called "festejadors", referring to possible courtship.

Related to thick or thin walls, not many years ago I was surprised by the Dutch engineers, who were collaborating with us in converting a heritage building, a former, brick built,

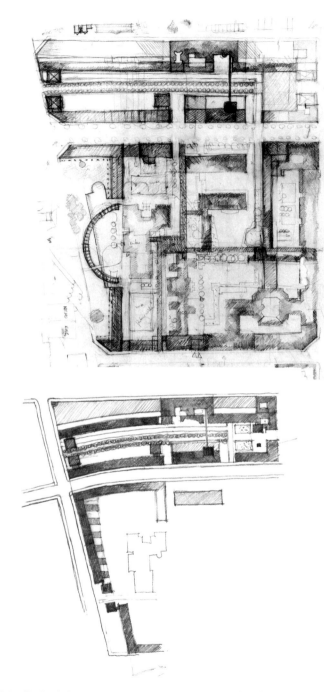

IBA Urban Design 1, Südliche Friedrichstadt, Berlin, Germany (1981)

trade school into government offices in the frontier town of Heerlen. They pointed out that the extensive glass wall we had proposed for the additional floor, marking the difference between new and old, needed to be adjusted to the legal requirements limiting the size of the window-wall to conserve thermal insulation. In the summer this meant keeping the interior temperature four degrees lower than the exterior, thus avoiding the necessity of air conditioning, at least in Holland. The solution was to add fixed louvers for shade.

Our solution begs the question of why did we not stick to ordinary windows? The answer lies in the objective of distinguishing the restoration of the original school from the new. This has always been the case throughout the history of architecture. Observe the different styles of different periods when the cathedrals and churches in Europe were extended. This subject is one of the most fascinating problems of architecture. It is not easy to isolate aspects of architecture. Every part of the process of design and construction of a building is related to a whole, very similar to the game of chess where each piece has its own move but this has to relate to other pieces on the board. The thin walls, almost obligatory today for economic reasons, have lost the strong demarcation of space between the inside and outside of the wall. However there are ingenious ways of overcoming this disadvantage.

Probably one of the earliest examples can be found in the dormer window that protrudes from the slope of the roof. These allow people to stand upright, close to the window. The solid sides form the transition between the inside of the attic and the outside. The combination of the slant of the roof and the vertical geometry of the dormer establishes an attractive, tent-like, space. Sometimes, when the attic is not in use, the light creeping into the loft from dusty glass makes it mysterious space. No doubt for many of us, when a loft or attic is used as a store, it recalls our childhood imagining of lost treasures.

The above example is restricted to attic rooms. However by turning the thin walls outwards, or inwards, on any floor level, like a glazed tribune, or a bay or bow window, we can also increase the space between the inside and outside with extended jambs.

I first noticed this in the mid-fifties, when as a student in Barcelona I visited the crypt of the unfinished church in the *Colonia Güell* by Antoni Gaudí and his collaborators, designed and built in the first decade of the 20th Century. The irregular folding zigzag plan of the enclosing wall (the same way you make a plain sheet of paper stand up) is pierced with glazed oval-windows within triangular hooded jambs that jut in and out of the thin wall. In this case the jambs are exterior and glazed with a majority of white tiles to reflect the northern light through the coloured abstract patterns of the glass, designed by Gaudí's assistant, Jujol.

About the same time, but in London, I noticed small triangular windows that jutted out. These appeared, now and again, amongst the more expensive suburban houses, probably introduced during the Arts and Crafts period, around the turn of last century. There was one in the house where I rented a studio-bedroom in Highgate in North London while studying architecture. This may explain my interest in these curious oriel windows.

We have been looking at the windows as the source of light and ventilation that pierce the protecting wall between the inside and outside. They also have another important role in presenting the whole building as part of the city, what we might call its public role. The composition of windows on the main façade, facing the street, is part of the city, town, or village itself. The outer face of a building is no longer exclusively private property because it goes towards creating the character of the street itself, which is a public domain, shared with others.

Sometimes this public role is particularly hard for the owner of a building to understand. He having paid for the building, believes it is his, exclusively, forgetting that in the first place he, or she, has had to obtain permission to build from his co-citizens, through their elected representatives.

Nothing is quite so simple. Not all citizens, or their representatives, are aware of their cultural responsibilities to the community and importance of the quality of the heritage to be left for future generations. When this responsibility fails and allows the owners to do what they like or when there is no cultural debate, this indicates an imbalance of power in favour of the individual, placing the architectural structure of the city in jeopardy.

The architecture of buildings and cities involves politics as well as culture.

Generally, in the past, façades have either followed the craft of building and the discipline of the street, or the more codified language of the classical. The need for abundant social housing after the First World War was too rapid to produce an accepted discipline that acknowledged its civic responsibility. True the tiny Modern Movement in Architecture and Urban Design did show its head in Berlin, Amsterdam and some other European cities. However it has been almost suffocated by the rise of the commercial so called Modern Style which threw overboard the cultural, social and respectful technological aims of the Modern Movement itself.

The above reflections lead us back to the arrangement of windows today. This is not only about thin walls, and the window itself, but also about setting up the composition of windows for a façade. Architectural composition is a complex process. One example in which I was personally involved was in the late fifties. A local cooperative, organised by a group of friends, asked us to design the first phase of an urban street block facing one of the main avenues of Barcelona, the Meridiana.

Economy and quality was required for as many three-bedroom dwellings that could be accommodated within the restrictions of the site, but with a view to future phases of construction as an increasing number of clients joined the cooperative. The initial site could extend on both sides. At that time in Spain economic construction was limited to load bearing walls which could only sustain a building of eleven stories with reduced floor spans. To squeeze the required number of dwellings together resulted in long narrow rooms, facing the façade.

It was my task to make a proposal for the façade. Faced with an empty white sheet of paper on my drawing board, the challenge was to decide which window form would raise the quality of light needed for narrow rooms. The second challenge was to compose a dignified façade for a development of apartments that were all the same.

Creative architecture calls for strategic thinking, like chess. So it was necessary to decide which piece to move first. To illustrate this analogy I have illustrated the opening moves in a game of chess.

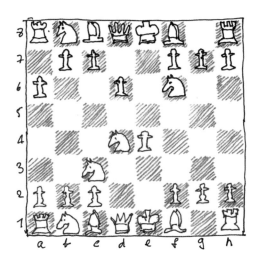

Chess remains the finest education of the mind requiring the tranversality between the rational and the unlimited imagination that can accompany our lives.

1. Pawn to king four, to command the central space (W white)

A classic opening, almost ordinary, dull but safe, like the anodyne rows of identical windows and empty urban terraces waiting for a spark of humanity to establish an identity.

Somewhere in my visual memory I associated the simple pawn with the almost insignificant oriel window based on an elongated triangular form. The street façade faced due West from where the mid-afternoon sun could penetrate the home, like the matador's sword in Hemingway's *Death in the Afternoon*. The windows needed their own "muleta", to defend them from the cruel five-o'clock heat. If we blocked out one half of the triangular window, the one facing North-West, the window would have its "muleta", leaving the open South-West to welcome the earlier, more vertical, sun into the narrow

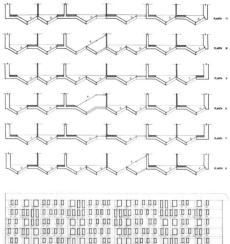

Architecture has been referred to as the "Mother of all Arts", so sometimes it is able to incorporate the inspiration of music and the ballet of chess.

rooms glancing off the inner side of the solid jamb to enliven the interior space.

Remembering Pete Seeger's fascinating song, based on Malvina Reynolds words, criticising these "little boxes" that people are forced to live in, I realised that I was on the same track as Pete. It was imperative to find a different functional composition of the windows, responding not to the identical plans, but to the diversity of the families who were going to live there.

True the unusual form of the protruding V-shaped window from the non-structural, thin, wall would in itself cause a rippling effect of shadow across the façade, but the regimented order would still be there.

2. King's knight to f-three, recovering White's control of the centre (W)

By now one can see that architecture, like chess, counts simultaneously on different elements (or pieces) that relate to an identical space. Variations of the cill heights were necessary between the living-room with a lower cill, allowing one to see out from a sitting position and the bedrooms with a higher cill to give more freedom for the distribution of the furniture. This provided us with two elements or pieces to play with.

2. Queen's pawn to d-six, commanding more of the centre and allowing a Bishop free to attack (B)

What we had now in the composition of the façade were two parallel vertical lines of bedroom windows and two parallel vertical lines of living room windows per dwelling. However, since they were symmetrically related to one staircase they would be perceived to be four vertical lines of each type. Having assembled all the pieces, it was now a question of how

to break the monotony, introducing a rhythm related to the order that had been established.

3. Queen's pawn to d-four, challenging Black (W)

This is the magic moment when architecture approaches music and begins to compose the façade, with variations on a theme, choosing a rhythm with a divertimento, with the intention of arriving at a harmonious whole.

3. Pawn takes Pawn to weaken White's centre (B)

Up till now the functional needs of the interior are expressed on the outside of the wall.

We have the notes but not the music.

4. Knight takes pawn leaving White in a strong position (W)

The proposal was to use a contrary, contrapuntal motion of two melodic lines, keeping the adjoining vertical lines of bedroom and living-room windows stable to contrast with a one-two-three alternative interlocking rhythm, set between separate and adjoining positions of the two remaining windows. In chess terms the movement follows the way a Knight can move: that is in any direction, moving two squares, flying over the first and then landing diagonally onto the next, either right or left.

4. Knight to f-six threatening White's central pawn (B)

Since I was dealing with architecture the idea had to be drawn to communicate to the builder, and of course for myself to see what the result was.

5. Knight to c-three bringing a second Knight to the centre and protecting White pawn (W)

Since the eleven floors chop off the rhythm it is continued in the next staircase. I have to confess that there are at least three errors, one by myself and two by the builder, but nobody notices as the rational attempt to produce an apparently free and loose composition was achieved.

5. Pawn to a-six preventing White Bishop's strategic attack[1] (B)

The Meridiana façade has been described in detail, to demonstrate that getting the façade right is no simple task. However this is an unusual exception to the normal effort to fit the clothing of a new building to the body of its existing neighbourhood, either the urban street or the countryside. Such an approach is only appropriate when the environment appears to be negative, or requires punctuation. This role is generally reserved for institutional architecture. However a domestic use can also assume this role like Palladio's *Palazzo Thiene Bonin Longare* in Venice (if we admit that a palace is domestic), or Rietveld's *Schröder House* in Utrecht at the end of a row of undistinguished houses, marking both the end of the row, and the abrupt right hand turn of Prins Hendriklaan street into a country lane.

Both are rather weak examples of urban intentions as their architects were concerned with other areas of investigation. On the other hand, Barcelona's Puig i Cadafalch's *Casa de les Punxes* marks an unforgettable domestic image along the Diagonal at a complex street junction, as Gaudí did with the *Casa Milà* and *Casa Batlló* in passeig de Gràcia. J.A. Coderch and M. Valls also signalled an important street corner with their *Casa dels Pescadors* in Barceloneta.

In Madrid the classic example of a domestic monument can be found just at the moment Barajas expressway meets the city's urban street system. F.J. Saenz de Oiza's *Torres Blancas*, a metropolitan landmark, is a vertical homage to the American architect Frank Lloyd Wright, whom he admired.

The three façades of the most sophisticated building ever built serve as urban punctuation in the extreme heritage context of Vienna. Neither institutional nor domestic, but paying homage to both, A Loos' *Looshaus* in Michaelerplatz, built in 1910, was, at first, the object of public outrage. The façades were divided into two halves: the lower half combined historical references in stone with proportionally large windows. The upper half presented a stark modern appearance with a contrasting white wall with simple square windows along the three sides of the remaining four floors. To appease the public the city architects insisted that flower boxes, with flowers, be added beneath some of the square windows to mitigate the severity of the geometry of the upper half. Hopefully one day they will be removed.

Pyrenees (sketchbook), Valaria d'Orient, Andorra (1983)

Abbey on the banks of the Danube (sketchbook), Melk, Austria (1984)

Cascading stream (sketchbook), Vall d'Incles, Andorra (1984)

1 *The popular Sicilian Defence with the Najdorf Variation that can lead to a strong control of the centre*

Our holiday home with friends (sketchbook), Ransol, Andorra (1984)

For the citizen strolling through the streets of his city, town or village, the buildings have many stories to tell, many intriguing, but too often dull and disappointing. Opportunities lost?

Façades contain more challenges than windows, like the corner between two walls, like the west front of a cathedral and its side walls and windows, or how the ground floor addresses the street level, the way the façade meets the skyline, or perhaps most important of all, defining the main entrance.

Can We Ignore Examples of History?

The context of the façade has just been mentioned. This indicates the value of understanding the past and questions if we can really ignore the examples of history, or archaeology, if we wish to critically examine buildings themselves and their contribution to the ever changing city. Often the new contains a reference to the past, since the problems of composition have always been a similar task for architects. The time-line of a city is much longer than ours.

Our own time has led us into the Age of the Image. Our eyes see through the mind that frames what we look for. A window that is too often subjected to other flickering images that feed our imagination. They are manufactured by others so we have to learn how to filter them with our own knowledge. Television is a technical marvel that few of us have the courage to reject. More invidious is the invasion of public space with the constant inclusion and repetition of the image of advertisements, compelling you to notice something you are not really interested in and clouding your right to contemplate what you chose.

Advertisements are the most significant visual contaminants. We see commercial images on roofs, façades, on public transport, in stations, airports, in front of trees and flowers, in fact, everywhere. We cannot look inside a bank or open a newspaper without the screaming messages that continue their bombardment through the radio waves around us.

Fortunately we have the ability to constantly adjust ourselves to difficult circumstances and turn a blind eye to the repetitive vulgarity in most of the ever expanding cities around the world. Perhaps there are moments we can learn to find a lost beauty amongst the shock of all this vulgarity. It may even be stimulating to some.

When I was a fresh architect with my degree still in my pocket, I was fortunate to meet an elderly lady, an architectural historian, who told me it was so much better never to read a guidebook before visiting a city. Just enjoy getting lost and discover it. Afterwards compare your own adventures with

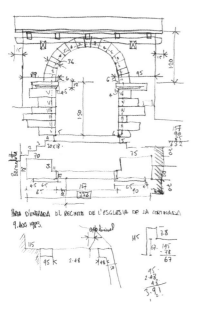

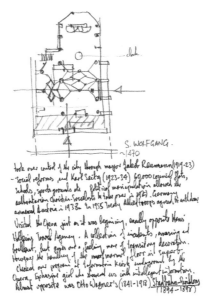

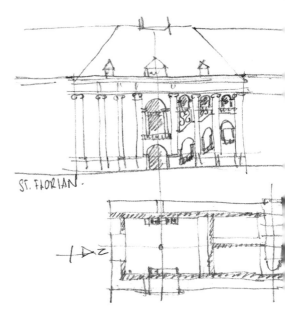

Lych gate (sketchbook), La Cortinada, Andorra (1983)

Plan of St. Wolfgang (sketchbook), Vienna, Austria (1984)

Augustine Monastery St. Florian (sketchbook), Vienna, Austria (1984)

the guidebook to fill in the dates, name of places and notable authors.

My own first voyage of architecture began on a bicycle when I was sixteen, along the rolling countryside of the upper Thames, near the Goring Gap. It was my last year at the Benedictine boarding school when our English literature teacher suggested, just before the Easter holidays, that I could bring my bicycle to school to visit some of the parish churches to learn about architecture and prepare for the Final School Certificate examination at the end of the summer term.

"Cuthbert Smith, our teacher, was one of those rare teachers who conveyed with ease what he wanted his pupils to discover. After visiting one parish church after another, we learnt about the process of construction and how buildings developed through changing social demands, increasing wealth and new aesthetic ideas. The delight of field work, rather than books, opened a whole new world for me.

From reflecting on the churches we visited, we realised that each generation, when called upon to extend the church, or renovate part of it, did so according to the customs, fashions or building techniques available at the time. In other words, they never imitated past styles. This only began to change in the 19th century, a period in architecture later known as the "battle of the styles". Nowadays, most architects express their own epoch, the zeitgeist of their own age, rather than reproducing earlier styles. It is a pity that the general public tends to feel surer with the old rather than the new.

Cuthbert Smith connected literature and architecture and I wanted to go on with both. The separate subjects we were taught by separate teachers and examined upon by others were suddenly no longer separate. Architecture seemed to unite them all. Geography, social history, geometry, physics, etc. were all there in the stones, timber and glass of the parish churches"

(from *A Life in Cities*, an architectural autobiography by the author, RIAS 2009)

Looking and Discovering

Sharing these memories may help to explain how personal experience of the simple art of looking and wondering what we are looking at, can give us the pleasure of discovering how much we can learn or even confirm the ideas we already have. This is part of the constant exercise of reviewing the reality around us.

I am sure that all of us, at one time or another, have sat on a bench in a park or in a bus or train, just watching the world go by. If we have been there before, travelling across town and country, we are comforted, recognising familiar objects that tell us where we are as time and space slip by. But why have we selected these objects of ours, and not others, to keep in the library of our memory? Have we ever asked this question?

Our visual impression belongs to us, and us alone. Printed or projected images are of course shared with others, and can even lead to a confusion with our own personal memories, especially when they are from early childhood, between the pages of a family album. Anyway, these visual memories, either personal or shared, are with us when our eyes explore the streets and squares and the buildings that make them. The complexity of our observation also depends on the moment of being. Empathy generally establishes itself with calmness. Remembering that our perception of architecture can only be enriched if we give ourselves time to think.

Our environment is not just the thrill of the wildness of nature. There is so much more to be found in the history of the artificial: man made environment, of our agriculture, the architecture of the landscape or garden, and the architecture of the urban settlements and their buildings. They are, in a way, an extension of the clothes we and other people wear, be they fitting and elegant, or just thrown on, without any special care. This brings us back to the views that people, landscapes and buildings show of themselves, what we see as we sit on a bench to watch the world as a stage. But beneath the outer garments of people, landscapes and buildings there is the underwear of form and function, processed through structure and materials and the life lived within.

Our Clothes: Representation and Comfort

It is interesting to note that the contrasts in fashion are similar to those in architecture. We are either tightly fitted or loosely draped in clothes. Architecture can similarly be loose fit or constrained. Both are often connected with outside events. Napoleon's expedition to Egypt introduced a strong oriental air, with women wearing little and extremely décolleté, vaguely transparent, while architecture responded mainly with decorative motifs.

Much of this Egyptianising tendency can be seen in memorials, in cemeteries. But I still remember the *Carreras CigaretteFactory* in Camden Town which I cycled by each evening on the way to the *Northern Polytechnic*. Its granite Egyptian columns, marching along the glass façade, were a wonderful example of solving the problem of scale. In Barcelona the *Casa Bruno Cuadros* in the Rambla, reformed by Josep Vilaseca, stops many tourists to photograph its oriental façade. Antoni Gaudí's *Casa Vicens*, with its opium smoking room, fits custom and architecture close together. Perhaps the *Carreras Factory* was actually referring to the ancient origins of drugs.

There is No Longer Only One History

Today there is no longer any one fashion, either in clothing or architecture. Among the variety is the curious development of clothing buildings all over with a diaphanous material, presumably to reduce the glare of strong light or temperature control. One might suspect that the architect is searching for a minimalist effect for a sexy aesthetic reason. Anyway it is worthwhile discovering what lies behind the design of buildings and to note the decorative impulse as "man in his time plays many parts".

The built images around us tell us something about the social, cultural and technical voyage of architecture through time and place. That is, if we care to look and consider. This exercise bridges the gap between "separate" subjects that make the tales of history coherent.

The use of the word "tales" is important. History is almost always interpreted according to the values of the moment it is being recorded in and so is open to critical examination. The history of architecture demands critical attention which can be enhanced by the adventure of personal discovery and questioning, rather than just leaving one to be informed by guide books. Even the experts have to be questioned.

We split history into periods, like the classics, Greek and Roman, the more obscure Medieval, the early, middle and late Renaissance, when the revival of ideas of classical antiquity,

basically Roman, based on a modular system of proportion, also implied the freedom to question everything in life. This was followed, to the limits of bacchanalia, in the Baroque and later the riot of Rococo, leading to the spiritual meditation of Georgian architecture, precursor to the 19th century battle of styles, during the Industrial Revolution.

Meanwhile, the rationalism of engineering and new technology led the way into the 20th century, along with the more romantic Arts and Crafts, looking to the customs of ordinary domestic living, no doubt influenced by the enlightenment of the increasing role of women. It was a moment for change and many turned to the examples of nature for inspiration, more decorative than structural, more feminine and softer than the heavy industry and commerce of men.

Modern architecture began to appear with the incorporation of rational design and the concern for civic and social sensitivity. However, the real nerve of history lies in between the current definition of these recognised set periods of architecture: the moments of change and doubt. It is here where we find the risk of extreme creativity in the effort to

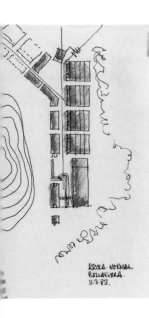

Urban design. Faculty for teachers, University Autonomous, Bellaterra, Barcelona, Catalonia (1983)

Social housing, Kochstraße, Berlin, Germany (1985)

define a new vision of architecture. The pulse of history quickens in times of a challenge to the prevailing social and cultural status quo.

Spaces and Places

Time itself is an essential part of history, recording changes in many spheres of life. However this is no less important than the place where something happened.

Visiting a museum of rural history I stopped in front of a text which explained in a nutshell just what was going around in my head, not yet resolved to become a coherent thought. I snapped out my mobile telephone and photographed the text which I reproduce below, with permission from the authors of the exhibition,

"From the tie between persons and the spaces that surround them are the places, because places are the spaces where persons are, have been or wish to be. When the relationship between people and places becomes firm and close, a very definite landscape arises, and since the links between persons and their places are different, so is each landscape."

I thought this so very true that it could be applied just as well to the built environment of the city or town wherever we live. The brief text added something about the timeline of history.

"The appearance of landscape is highly influenced by the morphological, physical, ecological and political traits of a territory, but it also depends to a large extent on the esteem in which they are held by the people who inhabit them."

If this is true of landscapes, then it is also true of cityscapes. Cities, towns and villages, and even the single house, have all adapted to the conditions of space becoming a place, throughout the history of architecture. Only in our own times do uncontrolled economic values tend to ignore geography and climate with the promise that technology can dominate all. Just as those who were confident that the Titanic was invulnerable when it set sail in 1912. But perhaps what was more significant was that only the first class passengers were saved, too similar to the present economic crisis.

Money is necessary but ideas come first. Extravagance can destroy elegance and empty the purse in the long run. Even sustainability has to consider the limits of the available finance when technology promises a golden future. The important question is to balance custom, moulded through time, with the uncertainty of new discoveries.

I remember with relief how this question came to mind when I left the London architectural offices in the late fifties, full of industrial catalogues of metal windows that standardised façades. I exchanged them for discussions with local artisans in their workshops when I came to Spain. We could apply their knowledge to what we were designing and solve problems, addressing cultural, social and technical demands. Spain was just starting to move on from the civil war, a time that was grey, difficult but exciting. I found similar situations later in East Germany and Poland at the time that the infamous Berlin Wall came down.

The Many Lessons of the Past

Some things do not change; time can also be put aside. We can still enjoy a Mozart piano concerto, like the slow second movement in no. 21, or the popular bounce of Vivaldi's *Four Seasons*, or the innocent, brilliant rhythms and poetry of the Beatles.

Music is a culture allied to architecture, but so is painting (I often look to Joan Miró for a curve), sculpture (the elongated

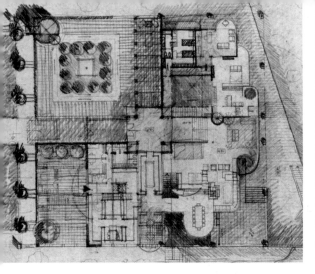

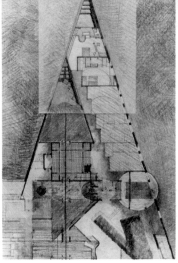

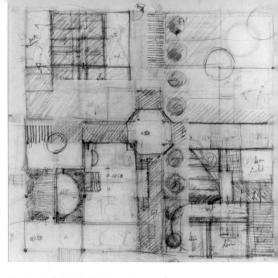

Mansion 2, Principal floor, Son Vida, Mallorca, Balearic Islands (1985)

Mansion 2, Lower floor, Son Vida, Mallorca, Balearic Islands (1985)

Mansion 1 (after Palladio and Lutyens), Son Vida, Mallorca, Balearic Islands (1985)

forms of Giacometti inspire drama) or the value of the empty space in the theatre of Samuel Beckett. Not only the no-place but also the no-time in *Waiting for Godot*, reminds us of how often we find waiting people in the streets and corridors of our own lives. A pleasant place can alleviate the endless time for a bus to arrive or our name to be called out in a medical waiting room. Within all cultural disciplines historical references are always present.

In architecture references are relatively simple. Have you ever looked at a medieval cathedral to see how the corner is turned between the west front and the side aisles? Usually it is rather careless. Renaissance façades have vertical bookends, the rules established how to meet the ground and sky. We have the rugged base and the neat cornice, both defining the limits of the bit in the middle, where the columns or stone framed windows are set.

Going from the general to the particular. If you happen to be in Berlin, visiting the *Altes Museum* by the neo-classic architect Karl Friedrich Schinkel, apart from the spectacular entrance porch, observe how to turn a corner, at the back of the building, incorporating a rainwater pipe. The past has many design lessons for the present. It would be foolish to

ignore them. They are as valid today as they were yesterday. In the process of design and construction there are innumerable occasions of difficult design considerations that need time to resolve. These challenges recur in all epochs of architecture.

These are what we could call the consistent disciplines of architecture itself. How to turn a corner of a building is one example. When we move to the architecture of the city the corner introduces us to the meeting of two streets, where different things happen. You arrange to meet somebody, or enjoy a chance meeting with somebody else. The corner is also a place to wait.

Corners are an essential part of everybody's daily life in an urban settlement. In a way a street corner almost defines what a city is about: the dynamic quality of the urban space, where different experiences are lived and learned. They provide the punctuation in the constant moving through the streets by foot, bicycle and vehicle, the heartbeat of a city that is alive, quite different from the relaxed formality of the public square.

The Importance of Corners

Turning a corner is the way we learn how to move through the city or indicate the way when asked. Even within a building we indicate the way "turn right and it's the third door on your left". We like to select a table in the corner of a restaurant. In years gone by, now I hope very seldom, a child is told to go and stand facing the corner.

Many critical places in sport are corners, boxing and football, for example. They are also a place of refuge where one can defend oneself better. Buildings often have a window running round a corner or an enclosed gallery, not only to capture the view but also the changing light as the day slips by.

The corner is protective but it can also be threatening. Urban warfare makes corners both a shelter and a danger. In films the corner is chosen for comedy and drama, the Gog and Magog of the theatre. Nothing illustrates this better than Carol Reed's film from the novel by Graham Greene when Holly Martins waits around three tilted corners in Vienna for black-marketeer, and ex-school friend, Harry Lime, played by Orson Welles. The tension, the haunting music, and the corners, enlarged by the dark oblique photography, mixed with the humour of Harry Limes' entrance and exit, proves the importance of the corner.

The Devil is in the Joints

One day I was showing the legendary Estonian architect Louis Kahn around a school we had designed. On the way in, going up the courtyard steps, he stopped and stooped, digging his finger into an unfinished joint, "The secret of good architecture lies in its joints, this one was not well done". I agreed. This particular one was not finished, but I got the message. He was a grand old man of architecture and I was still learning.

Buildings are full of joints, doors and their frames, walls with their ceilings and floors, the wooden floors themselves, tiles in bathrooms, and of course furniture (everyone knows how many joints there are when you arrive back home from Ikea). There are others that need thinking about if you have little experience, joints in the roof could let the rain in, the joint between different materials or elements like roof and chimney, and joints within the structure, be it steel or concrete. Then there are the thermal joints, every thirty metres. Joints are important in construction and aesthetics. They are not easy to resolve.

If you look carefully you will notice how joints are made, or covered. Joints move according to the temperature, humidity and the way different materials expand and contract. Many people do not realise that buildings are alive, materials are not dead, that's why we see cracks or hear strange noises at night.

Decoration was born, in part, from the need to cover moving joints, the plaster cornice between the wall and ceiling, the skirting between the wall and floor. Then there is a question of vibration from traffic, wind, rain, and the ground itself, resisting weakness and earthquakes.

Just as our bodies suffer with changes in climate and age, joints need care. A little three-in-one can ease the squawking hinge or a difficult lock, but not every joint has an easy solution at hand.

Louis Kahn's warning that the secret of good architecture lies in the joints was directed not only at the construction of buildings, but also the composition of form.

Lazy Architecture

If architecture has its own particular discipline we can ask why do some architects turn out lazy architecture that tends towards vulgarity, often unrelated to setting. Apart from a lack of professional care, the powerful building industry, with political support, has recently grown to dominate the urban scene. Investment banks have lost the direct contact with knowledgeable builders and professional sub-contractors. These specialists are now replaced by accountants and lawyers, apparently representing the banks, who appear at the first meeting with the lead contractor.

Contract managers are appointed by corporate clients to

ensure minimum costs. In a way all this is understandable. But it can easily lead to poor workmanship and changes in the quality of the architecture itself, on the insistence of the contractor, which can lead to expensive ongoing maintenance for the client.

The corporate client seldom has a cultural face and is often obsessed with emotional architecture, the so called "wow factor", delivered by a popular "starchitect" of the moment and their meeker followers, who cost less. Unfortunately public commissions are not immune from this disease, in spite of bureaucratic competitions with almost unseen juries. There are of course exceptions because there is still a gallant rear-guard in the building industry, that value work well done, protecting the retreating skilled professionals and all of the team.

The Architecture of Movement

"Safe as houses", is a common phrase, indicating the economic stability of buildings. Naturally buildings are expected to resist the elements and define their internal and external spaces for the use of their inhabitants and visitors. This is why the client draws up a list of rooms to be incorporated into the design.

There is of course a lot more to it. I found this confirmed when visiting the architect Denys Lasdun in his office in London. It was shortly after I had met him in Barcelona when he gave a lecture at the school of architecture. To my surprise he also visited the Civil Governor who represented Franco, to inquire after a Catalan political prisoner and ask for his release on behalf of Amnesty International. I realised how little we know sometimes about the humanity and generosity of people we think we know.

Denys was explaining to me about the new building for the *College of Physicians*, facing Regents Park, which I had just visited. He had the list of rooms from the client and that was all. So he had reminded his client that, apart from the corridors, there was the entrance and staircases that also had a representative role, and were in fact very necessary, not only

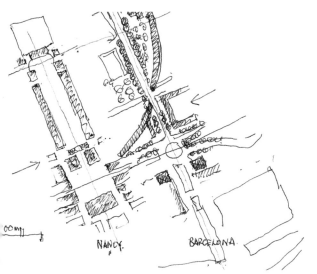
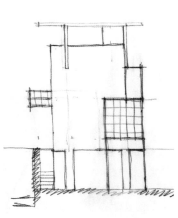
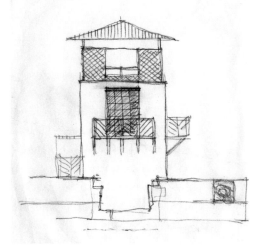

History is always a good companion: it remains in the memory.
The movement opening Barcelona to the sea
builds up the theatrical sequence inspired by Nancy

Artist studio towers 1 & 2, Son Vida, Mallorca, Balearic Islands (1985)

for access but also to orientate the people using the building. When it was built the finest spaces were the vestibule and staircase, still the pride of the *College*.

This was in the mid-sixties when C.P. Snow published his novel *Corridors of Power*, set in the world he knew –the corridors and committee rooms of Whitehall. The blurb on the back of my Penguin edition goes on to state that rarely has the manipulation of political power been handled with such authenticity and intimacy by an author. Snow had become a civil servant during World War II. His principal character in the book is a Parliamentary Secretary, Roger Quaife. Brilliantly honest, Quaife declares: "The first thing is to get the power. The next is to do something with it". Fortunately in the novel he needed his power to oppose weapons of mass destruction. This episode brings us close to the importance of chance contacts along the corridors and lobbies through which people need to move.

A chair, a table and a room of your own allow you a place and a time to think, write or draw. Movement allows you to gather unexpected information. Not for nothing Washington has its lobbies. Not for nothing do cities have markets, squares, buildings with corridors and the streets that lead to them.

Our bodies depend on the circulation of the blood, our brain on the circulation of ideas. Our homes are enriched with alternative ways of reaching a room. Learning in school depends not only on the classroom but also circulating along the internal 'streets', the corridors where experience is acquired through chance encounters.

The late Baroque probably gives us the best examples of movement in architecture. The sequence of urban rooms in Nancy: a square, then a tight collar, and then again through the archways of a transverse hall to the long, tree lined, public place, finishing with another transverse forecourt, enclosed by circular columns. Our own, more modest finish to Barcelona's Marina Street, leading to the open sea through the Olympic Village, was inspired by Nancy. The well-known sequence of urban spaces in Bath, between the Circus and Crescent, is another skilful way of enticing movement through urban spaces.

The *Soane Museum* in London, displays the play of space and light as one is led to discover one surprise after another. Good for entertaining but perhaps a little too exotic for actually living in.

In the *Residence* in Würeburg, staircases probably occupy the largest space in the Palace and were meant to impress through the social movement of people wishing to be seen. The *Paris Opera* staircase became almost a rule for theatres and concert halls across Europe.

These are all exaggerated examples of how to enrich the emotional experience of moving through a city or public building. Even in a small domestic house the angles of vision, an axis or diagonal, can create emotional pleasure, inviting changing views and playing with the quality of natural light.

The visitor experiences the space between what is public and private when approaching the front door. This is a hierarchical process towards the intimacy, protection and privacy of the inside. It is not necessarily anti-social. Although a barrier to some, the door, at the same time can be inviting and welcoming for friends. Balance in the process is what is called for.

The separation of the building from the street with a garden allows time to cushion the arrival for both resident and visitor. When this is not possible, steps, or a ramp, create a difference in levels which signals the approach. A porch in front of the door provides shelter and allows the resident to observe the caller from a window. When residents leave the building the steps allow a pause to observe what is going on in the street. This is a typical architectural solution to the entrance of a mid-18th century European town house, more elaborate for wealthy merchants and reduced to a necessary minimum in poorer working class districts.

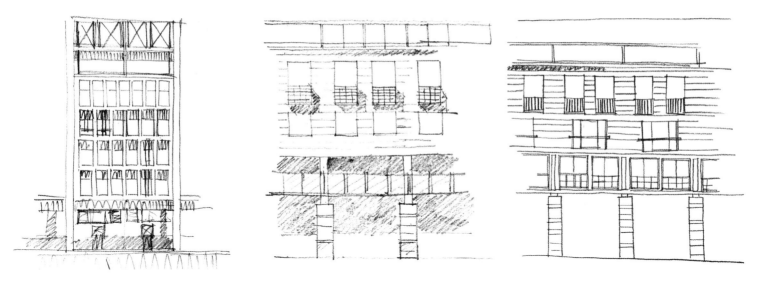

Housing, Pamplona, Navarra (1986)

The medieval internal courtyard allowed the owner to enter or leave his or her carriage away from any danger in the street. An external staircase then led to the front door on the first floor, known as the principal floor. The servants' kitchen and storage would occupy the ground floor: the upstairs and downstairs of social separation. Within the house, manor or palace, there would always be a separation between the servers and the served in passages and staircases, with the servants sleeping in basements or under the roof.

Other architectural elements can soften the severity of the entrance: by introducing glass, by painting the front door with a bright colour, like in Dublin, or by providing a vestibule that allows you to see through the building to the courtyard or garden beyond. All these little architectural details encourage confidence in where you are going. That is how architecture assists the perception of movement in space.

This hierarchy of entering is culturally strongly tied to the European manner which is surprisingly absent in the United States. For example, I entered a library in *Harvard University* opening the door directly to the reading room –there was no lobby or vestibule. I think everyone has noticed in Hollywood films how people often enter a house directly into the living area and then step down three or four steps, like coming off a stage in a theatre, but then perhaps that's what it is all about.

Generally, movement through any building should be guided by the architecture itself, indicating alternative routes through the punctuation of space with a lobby, different ceiling heights, playing with natural light and views outside so that you can relate to the city itself. Large buildings, government departments, museums, shopping centres and airports should provide signage with clear articulation of the movement of people to avoid frustration. Confusion, however, is often exploited where commerce tries to detain the possible client, especially in airports.

When entering a formal space, say a church, an assembly hall or even a lecture theatre, one can use the central aisle when the movement is informal, but tend to use the side aisles when the event is beginning or has already started. The hieratical space in a church is carefully established architecturally. The crossing of the nave with transepts, often accompanied with a higher dome that makes one pause before the choir stalls and altar, help to define religious moments in your movement through the enclosed space.

Traditional cities, towns and villages also have their hierarchical character, not necessary to define power, but also through the logical spatial guidance towards commerce and markets. Streets become more complex towards the centre and at least every five hundred metres there is an architectural punctuation, be it a building, a crossroads, a square or a pocket park. I found this out while I was redesigning a market to provide a missing place around it by removing structures that had accumulated through time.

It was in the city of Dublin. The object of our study was to create the mixed commercial focus of a traditional market place in this area which lay half way between the highly active O'Connell Street and the Smithfield horse market a kilometre away, linked directly by Mary's Lane that carved through a central area, falling into disuse.

Half a kilometre is just about as far as one is prepared to walk in a city to find the shop or restaurant you are looking for. You need to be encouraged with some kind of interest, a punctuation, in order not to give up the effort. It is worthwhile going out to see if this is true in your own city or town.

Till now the reform of the Dublin vegetable market has not been carried out. Smithfield is somewhat deserted, except for the weekend horse fair now and again. It is a great event and a very fine place, designed by good urban architects. However it is in need of strategic planning. The new tram line helps, but not enough.

The question which arises after the above comments on the architecture of movement is that we all move through our domestic and urban space in a way which is determined by the form of that space. A form that has occurred because other citizens, at one time or another, have made decisions according to personal and collective necessities. Our built environment

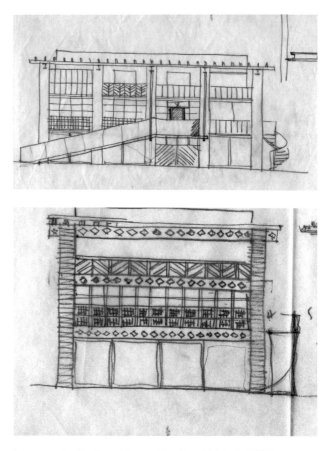

A house and a shop for gardeners, Barcelona, Catalonia (1987)

is historically present but seldom acknowledged as we move through these man-made, therefore, artificial spaces.

If there was more awareness we would perhaps be more critical. With more knowledge we might enjoy ourselves more. We could perhaps even participate as a client of our urban settlement, neighbourhood, or the city itself. A community, full of knowledge, could participate with a positive critical eye with a more open mind to question the future of our built heritage. Maybe we will have to leave this for future generations.

The city, town, village and countryside is ours, shared with others. Let us understand it and contribute with imagination and care, with constructive criticism, so that our elected representatives are aware of their cultural responsibilities for the places we all live in. Public places are, after all, public. This includes the public faces of the architecture that makes them.

The Gods of Proportion, Space and Light

Thomas Fuller, the 17th century English cleric and writer, was what we might now call an open progressive person. He remained a skilful commentator during Cromwell's civil war and after. He wrote, "Light (God's eldest daughter) is a principal beauty in building", in the context of citizens and the home. He could have had in mind the Greek mythology of Hyperion, the god of light and according to Homer, "Father of the rosy-armed Eos (dawn) and the rich blaided Selene (moon) and the timeless Helios (sun)". So if the Devil is in the joints, perhaps the gods lie in the quality and proportions of space and light.

Although we all live with light every day, we are not always aware that it has been a mystery for many during the past. Now with the initial conquest of space, we better comprehend light's relationship to time. It is explained to us that the stars we look at are not in our present time, making the speed of light difficult to grasp. Light is more than aesthetic, it lies deeply in the field of science. Antiquity believed that the eyes sent out rays of light like radar which bounded back to the eye and brain, the place where we perceive the image.

Ibn al-Haytham, known better as Alhazen, studying with the Fatimid caliphs in Cairo, around the year 1000, suggested that the phenomenon of light was just a simple one, that the eye just perceived the light and transferred it to the brain which translated it into an image. In this way, as reported in Julian Bell's critique in the *London Review of Books* on a publication by Hans Belting titled *Florence and Baghdad: Renaissance Art and Arab Science*, Alhazen devised the first known camera obscura.

This explains the probable cause why we do not all see the same image. It depends on the previous reserve of our memories which we draw on to interpret the image, and of course the physical state of our eyes. In other words we are all capable of giving a different opinion on the object we are looking at.

We tend to agree on what we see because the storage of knowledge that creates the image is in part determined by the culture we have been brought up in. However, this only becomes important when we are studying objects that were created in other cultures and other times. History is never exact, and light has a lot to do with it.

This could explain how we interpret the Islamic decorative forms of knot-patterns, honeycomb vaulting and lattice windows. As Julian Bell writes, "each invites us to acknowledge and contemplate, through line, a potentially endless multiplicity of foci", representing the transversability of the world itself. This supports the grand simplicity that anything we do or think is endlessly connected to everything else. Architecture is no exception.

We can note that architecture seldom ignores the proportional effects of natural light that changes, not only from dawn to twilight, but also during the course of the year and the state of the weather.

The quality of light is too rich for architecture to ignore. Light from my window is announced every day from below the horizon of the Mediterranean Sea where first it has lit the lands of Italy and Greece to the East. Each morning I draw the curtain to see the colour of the sea. It may be quiet, like a lake, or upset with the wind.

Colours change every minute and depending on the month we can sometimes see how the sun quickly flies from behind the water line to throw long gentle shadows from the buildings along from the shore side of the city. A shaft of warm sunlight lingers for a moment as we prepare for the coming day. Later we are distracted when the source of light is lost between the busy streets and low ceilings where we work or study.

The high ceilings of the past still allowed us to see the colour of the sky, still on a summer's day or with a fading light as a cloud passes by, unseen by many. We who live in the city, between its tall buildings, forget the sun and turn on the lights, their luminance adjusted to the papers on our desks. In winter mornings we leave to travel under the dark sky, the primordial power of the sunrise is diminished.

Natural light is a luxury for many. Even in tall buildings, springing upwards like a forest of trees seeking light, now hidden outside with tinted glass or netted screens –natural heat and cold and light are enemies to control. We are all bound to live at 23° Celsius and between 300 and 500 lux. But what has architecture done about using the magic of natural light, in the past and today?

Northern cathedrals are lanterns of captured light, filtered through tales told in coloured glass. In farm houses and city dwellings the rooms, depending on their use, are situated according to the time of the day. However, light is best dealt with when it is proportional to a desired effect, to increase the quality of the space.

Light has also to be seen in relation to the different moods of individuals at different times. This is well expressed by the poets. Within the same collection of poems from *Leaves of Grass*, Walt Whitman combines these shifting moods with:

"Give me the splendid silent sun with all his beams full-dazzling"

and follows this shortly with contrasting nature with the man-made scene:

"Give me faces and streets…
…give me the streets of Manhattan!"

In other words architecture also has to admit the perception if it aspires to be understood.

Photographers probably know more about natural light than anyone else. Even when trying to take a photo with any ordinary camera, or nowadays with a mobile telephone, the difficulty of finding the right light for the image takes time. Not all can be solved with technology because we have to select what we ourselves are aiming to obtain.

This is a particularly good way to begin to understand the façades and interiors of buildings. We become aware of shadows, receding doors and windows, the texture of materials, the reflections of glass and other polished materials. More frustrating is that we find the time of day is wrong and we may have to wait too long to get the light we wish for. This may be because the image looks dull when we know, or believe, that it would be more alive with the right light.

Photos inside a building are even more difficult because of the bright contrast of exterior light from windows, apart from the difficulty of capturing the essence of a small or complex space. This is overcome by professionals with high-tech digital cameras with a rapid sequence of shots, each image set with a different exposure.

We also may notice that the strong summer sun is less kind than the softer light of the spring or autumn. The low evening light is also mellower than the vertical light of the mid-day sun. Architecture takes all this into consideration. This is generally recognised by those who take photos of buildings and their streets or gardens and have time to gaze with empathy at their subject.

As we walk through alleyways or streets, turn a corner, find pocket squares or incidental gardens, we come to realise how the light encourages us to explore. If a dark space is

Olympic Village, coastline, Barcelona, Catalonia (1987)

Olympic Village, twin towers, Barcelona, Catalonia (1987)

Olympic Village, seafront porch, Barcelona, Catalonia (1987)

Olympic Village, beach and port, Barcelona, Catalonia (1987)

Olympic Village, courtyard gardens, Barcelona, Catalonia (1987)

not relieved by a distant light we hesitate to go further. No historic city has been designed without thought, either by custom or by a skilled architect. The skilled architect has the social experience to transmit to a drawing a sensibility to the proportions of space and light in the city and its buildings.

In Philadelphia, for example, there is a street with a wider pavement on the north side because it was beyond the shadow of the houses on the south side. In Berlin, the famous Karl Marx Alee has gardens on the north side. In Barcelona the extension of the Diagonal has a broad pedestrian walk, also on the north side.

Architecture has always played with light to enhance the quality of space from prehistoric monuments, through the theatrical effects of Baroque religious chapels, to the roof lights or skylights evolved through the technology of the industrial revolution. Indirect light, a necessity in art galleries, has now spread to various public buildings. Those who have visited Charles Rennie Mackintosh's *Glasgow School of Art* have experienced the complexity of its light. Few architects have so ingeniously exploited natural light.

The exploitation of light in architecture increases the pleasure to the enquiring mind of cities and buildings during the cycle of the seasons.

and all the
men and women
merely players

Olympic Village, beach freedom, Barcelona, Catalonia (1988)

Olympic Village, beach freedom, Barcelona, Catalonia (1988)

Can the Players Play Together?

"Tinker, tailor, soldier, sailor, richman, poorman, beggarman, thief", goes the nursery rhyme, usually played counting fingers and stopping on a finger selected before the game begins. This is meant to indicate which one you might be when you grow up.

This game introduces the unknown future and its casual effect on life to a young child. It probably has no lasting effect, except as an introduction to the delight of the world of the imagination.

Since these lyrics are a parody of something real, there is no reason why we cannot use them as a reference point for a consideration of the relationship between free choice and chance. This lyric is also a way of exploring the relationship between the citizen and the city, a city created through custom and intelligence, but also unexpected chance, for good or ill.

In the lyric the first group of four occupations are gathered together for their mobility, while the last four indicate a possible downward fall of fortune. Not a bad way of describing

the reality, or part of it, of the city. Its citizens may be trapped in a little box of fixed habits, assuming the present is permanent.

Decisions are made too often in little boxes of specialised activities, lacking the broader vision that can be gained from the various sectors of civil and public life necessary to evaluate the full implications of continuous change. The actors in a play each know the other's part, like the players in a successful football team. Such team working should also be present within the political and administrative structures of the city.

The greatest quality of a city is that it offers very wide choice. Different people bring different backgrounds and ideas and different products, be they of everyday necessity or of cultural value, are among these choices. The city provides both selected information and casual encounters with people and places. Multiple relationships within the city are generally missing in the structure of political decisions when concentrating a single use in one area. This gap can create false moves in the direction of city development. While the

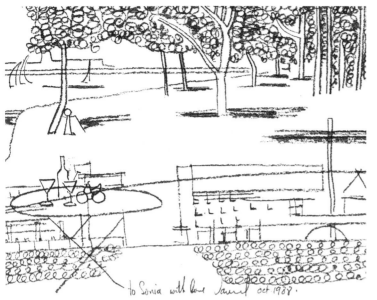

Olympic Village, park by the beach, Barcelona, Catalonia (1988)

Olympic Village, park by the beach, Barcelona, Catalonia (1988)

city may balance its past with the present, it is sometimes too ambitious about the uncertain future when changing reality may leave an infrastructure ill used or even abandoned.

Our nursery rhyme describes the constant movement within and between different activities. If this changing reality is not recognised it can cause more destruction than construction as has been mentioned before. The lyric also warns of economic consequences. Richman is two steps away from thief, although some might think of this as a vicious circle, bringing the thief too close for comfort to the rich man, a problem that could precipitate a social crisis through blatant corruption.

In the city, the players in question are, on one hand, the private sector of powerful developers, who were once builders, but nowadays are either investment banks or wealthy corporations. On the other hand is the public sector on tight budgets, often without the help of bank loans, for social construction. These are the possible clients for architects today. This is important because without a client an architect

cannot work. Or, as the Italian architect Vittorio Gregotti once commented to me, even with a client it is almost impossible.

Here there is even a dark side. The powerful building industry, through investment banks and giant engineering multinationals, offer contract packages for delivering "turn-key" finished buildings. This displaces the architectural profession which, according to some builders, saves on unnecessary fees.

It is true that many clients demand too much for the money available, or have already decided how they want their building to be. "L-shaped", said one client to me, another brought a series of illustrations from a glossy magazine of what looked like a dull suburban house from the U.S. Some just have a list of rooms and other requirements and then appoint a project manager to control the costs, having forgotten that the building needs an entrance hall, staircase and perhaps a corridor or two to connect the rooms.

In the public sector the client is often not an individual. So if architects are asked for proposals to design part of a city or one of its buildings, there is only a committee whose aim is to only agree on costs. Architecture is forgotten.

This difficulty reminded me of a Hungarian cartoon film. A painter arrived at a ministry H.Q. and asked what colour he should paint the waste paper bin. The hall porter phoned the maintenance department who consulted the secretary of the head of the department who then thought it should be the Minister himself, who was busy. The painter waited, then went out for a coffee.

Meanwhile the Minister listened to his secretary and asked her to consult a colleague from another ministry to know if there was a general government policy over colours for bins. The painter returned from his coffee, heard that there was no answer as yet, and hearing the hall-porter having doubts about any instructions till tomorrow, decided that green was best, set to work, finished the job and left. The cartoon finished there. The same situation could easily be found in the hierarchy of private corporations.

Many European cities now have culturally aware mayors or leaders who are sensitive to their responsibilities regarding the architecture of their city and its buildings. They take the place of the former city fathers, now that they democratically represent the citizens. However the problem of somebody having to make a decision may still lie further down in the administration. This is not to criticise any individual member, but it is a criticism of the lack of a clearly defined communication hierarchy.

For example, traffic engineers may dictate where the streets should be, but not how they look. Then the service engineers may decide where the accesses traps are, but not how they fit the joints in the stone paving. There may be regulations for the placing of rubbish bins. Then the rubbish bins may not be a comfortable size for elderly people to open. Too often there is a lack of clear communication between all those involved. Life is too rich to be reduced to separate disconnected objectives.

A civil servant is bound to explain a regulation but normally needs authority to interpret it. This is where easy communication is necessary. In Berlin, some years ago, I found that all the regulations were extensive and exact, providing for every known possibility. However we wished to include, at the base of a wall, a texture, introducing into the brickwork lines of flat ceramic tiles along the horizontal joints, and some alternative concrete blocks. This mix had not been foreseen. We were informed that a sample had to be sent to a laboratory to establish its strength to resist certain loads, and that would take a year or more. The custom of the builder to place weights (sacks of cement) to test it on site was not recognized by law. Laws if not looked after, fall behind the demands of reality and need fresh interpretation, now and again.

These of course are minor incidents, but they are an illustration of how serious situations that need decisions at higher levels do not work. This is true in city departments, local government, central government and the European Union itself, including cabinet meetings at the highest level. Political parties are not exempt. There are of course exceptions. I hope there will be more.

I was asked by a London architectural magazine to name the most important architect behind the preparations for the Barcelona Olympics. I had no hesitation in naming the Mayor, Pasqual Maragall. Anything to do with the architecture of the city and its buildings is 50% political and 50% professional. Political leadership, informed, cultural and imaginative, is fundamental to any city. Sometimes it will not be the leader themselves but somebody close. It all depends on the wisdom of the leader.

Streets Connect, Buildings Define, Squares Punctuate
The birth of a city and its foundation can be traced through two fields of investigation. First through the spiritual myths that are basically symbolic, together with legends that bind

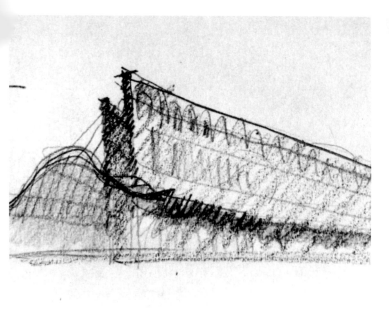

Expo Sevilla 92, Pavilion of the Future, Seville, Andalucía (1988)

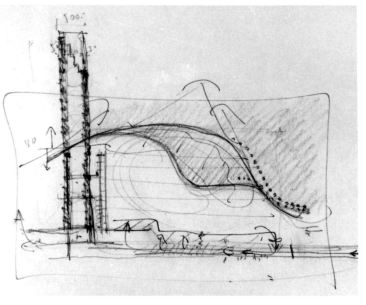

Expo Sevilla 92, Pavilion of the Future, Seville, Andalucía (1988)

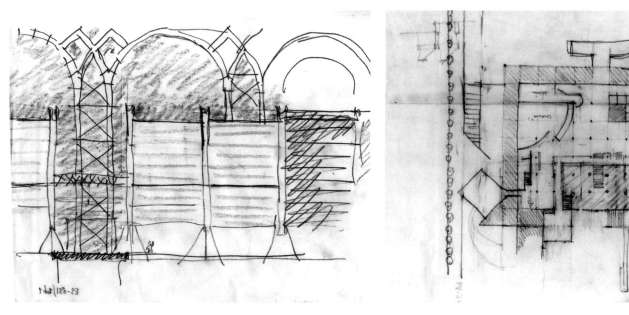

Expo Sevilla 92, Pavilion of the Future, Seville, Andalucía (1988)

Hotel lobby, Puerto Vallarta, Mexico (1988)

events into stories. Second, more rationally, through the findings of archaeology.

We can assume that discoveries in Mesopotamia and ancient Egypt indicate that there was a strong relationship between powerful leaders and the establishment of fortified settlements. However it would be a risk to assume that there was any recognisable pattern common to the different sites. On the other hand, prehistoric settlements, usually situated in strategic locations for protection and water supply, indicate the birth of a primitive street.

These early settlements follow a fairly regular pattern. One of the earliest I have seen was the spiral, 15 metre high, multi-storey, family dwelling called the Clickimin Broch, built with stone on a small island in the middle of a loch near what it is now the town of Lerwick in Shetland, Scotland. The building is claimed to date from 3.000 BC. I am not sure if this date refers to the building I saw, or an earlier one on the same site which was later extended. It is well worth a visit. Being on an island and just one large construction there is of course no reason for a street.

The earliest streets were more like paths and can be found in small settlements in Mesopotamia. They ran in between several patio dwellings, bounded by closely packed mud walls, enclosing a private farmyard. This street, or path, provided a link to the cultivated land and pasture beyond. Later, in Greek and Roman towns and cities, the streets were occupied with prosperous merchants and administrative classes, mixed in-between shops that had accommodation for tradesmen above.

The most accessible settlement to visit in Europe is probably Ostia, the port for Rome at the estuary of the Tiber, founded in the fourth century BC. The crossing of the two streets, Decumano Massimo with Cardine Massimo, formed the central Forum with its Capitolium and Temple of Roma and Augustus. Many of the houses reached three or four stories and many incorporated carefully designed façades to emphasise the wealth of the owners. I was surprised by Ostia because we are generally aware only of the layout of the foundations or single storey constructions. Many of these houses are impressive for their size in a city.

The street is the backbone of our society. Unlike the late "Iron Lady", Mrs Thatcher who said "there is no such thing as society", I believe that society is not solely about individual freedom. It is about the freedom to associate with others and to enjoy unexpected encounters. Such social encounters, planned or unplanned, allow for exchanges of information. This not only enriches our experience and knowledge, but provides a market place for cultural and commercial transactions.

The street gives a recognisable form to public space where people can seek out their markets and in the course of their search, acquire unexpected information – be it a product in a shop window or a chance meeting with a friend. Solutions to problems can often be triggered by an informal and unexpected encounter in the street, where people, unprotected by a ring of co-workers and an endless list of appointments, feel relaxed and able to discuss the real issue, not the official position.

In recent decades, a key reason for the decay in the quality of the public space and the street is a desire to avoid conflict. Herein lies one of the great misunderstandings about the configuration of urban settlements. The street of the town and city is alive only if it involves differences and conflict. It provides moments of opportunity, it is the basis of tolerance, the major instrument of civilisation.

To remove differences and conflicts and their concomitant opportunities for tolerance, is to strike a death blow to the vitality of the street. In social terms, the ghetto, or the gated estate, does not resolve conflict; it merely evades it. We all know that problems are not solved by avoidance. For example, when the street becomes monofunctional, say only for vehicles, a physical or visual barrier is created within the urban network and even isolates complete neighbourhoods.

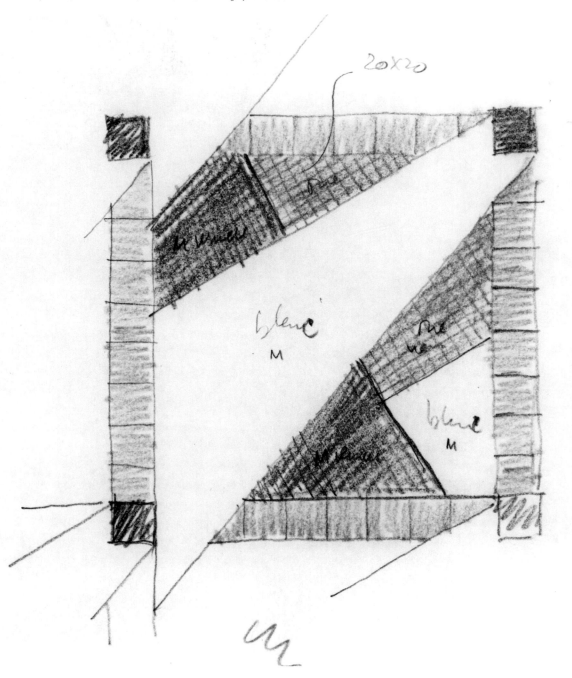

On the other hand, an excessive area of pedestrian streets, which may be successful shopping areas during the day, become unfriendly when deserted at night. One only has to observe how new restaurants, pubs and the occasional grocery shop are found along streets where vehicles pass by. Their presence gives a sense of security to pedestrians, and allows taxis to bring people to the restaurants and to enjoy the social vitality of the city.

It is now generally accepted that the functional city is a fallacy, yet highly infectious. Intellectual viruses still remain to destroy the fabric of the street. The most virulent is the virus of segregation. This classifies streets for specialised use, or in the case of vehicles, different speed limits, some so high that pedestrians are regulated behind barriers and hardly have time to cross from one side to another, with the permission of crossing lights.

On the other hand, areas of pedestrian only streets are welcome by day, and feared by night, from Cardiff to Cologne. The shopping mall, set in the centre of city blocks, leads to the closing of the shops facing the street, shutters down, boarded up ready for graffiti. In Milwaukee, in the eighties, I visited a mall which had converted part of the city centre into a ghost town.

Away from the existing street and inside the city block is the commercial imitation of streets. What saddens me most is the pathetic imitation of the life of the street inside the mall, with clowns and brass bands. Ominous security guards ensure that only appropriate people are allowed in. Traditional small shops, with all their rich variety and family care, are disappearing, leaving the hostile empty ground floors of our city centres questioning an uncertain future.

I suppose that severe winters, say in Canada, do not help street shopping. The traditional for protection from severe climatic conditions, both heat and cold, can still be found in the arcades of say Paris, Turin and La Seu d'Urgell in the Pyrenees, the glazed galleries of Cardiff, London and Milan.

Architects and other citizens who care for their city and its streets need to propose solutions like living workshops, dwellings for students and perhaps elderly people, professional offices or social services. It remains an unsolved urban problem because life styles are changing.

In West Ham, near the Lea Valley in London, close to the 2012 Olympic site, there are streets with high walls that followed the pedestrian pavements to protect the front gardens and dwellings behind. The street was deserted when I walked along it with no comfortable neighbourhood watch from the hidden houses. It was eerie and reminded me of the deserted paths next to the Berlin Wall. This street was an example of the slow destruction of what a city street is all about. The dwelling may be safer, the streets are not. When streets turn in on themselves and lead you nowhere, they do not invite you. Their weakness of public use makes them private.

The thought of Arcadia is tempting. It is one reason why the rich live in large country houses with extensive estates and landscaped grounds. Those from the middle class live in detached houses with a short drive up to the entrance. Those a little further down the social scale also live in separate houses, but instead of a front garden have a concrete car park. Further down the economic scale are regimented rows of identical houses, often semi-detached (to keep up with the detached). The poor live somewhere else.

The suburbs are half-way to the thought of Arcadia but one long step away from the city. This became confused in the garden-city movement with the idea of creating an urban countryside. It is a story that nearly everybody knows. The trouble began when developers drew up their own plans with winding streets that turn round on themselves. Every time one flies into Heathrow airport each developer plot can be

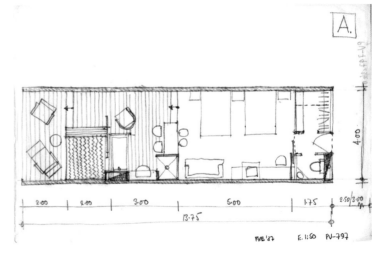

Hotel bedroom, Puerto Vallarta, Mexico (1988)

picked out by its street layout, similar but different to the one next door. Sub-urban is a good definition.

Street comes from the Roman "strata", road from the Old English, "rad", related to riding on horseback. Both indicate connections, which, too often in the suburbs, refuse to act as they should. Some say it is a safer road because you cannot drive through the area, so much so that, when you can, there is a road sign saying you cannot. Very odd and perhaps very English. But then I also found this discouraging tendency in Kreusburg in Berlin where the efficient Berliners eliminated the way through with roadblocks, apparently to allow children to play in the streets.

The principal function of the street is to connect. All settlements share the necessity to connect and communicate. This is the central theme that the Scottish biologist and town planner Patrick Geddes wrote about during the early years of the 20th century. A theme that social processes relate to spatial form which begins with the street.

Good connecting streets can be found in many of the model villages that sprang up in the latter part of the Industrial Revolution to improve the living conditions of the workers and their families. Outside Barcelona we have the so-called "colonies", attached to the mills along the river Llobregat. One such is the interesting *Colonia Güell* in Santa Coloma de Cervelló by Antoni Gaudí and his team of architects. It includes two streets, the school at one end and the cooperative shop at the other. Gaudí avoided axial dominance of the church by situating its crypt amongst the pine trees, slightly apart from the village.

The architectural history of any city can be felt and read as we walk through it. Barcelona is one of the clearest examples in which to sense and understand its changes in time and space. The Gothic city is clearly based on its Roman origins. The well-known street crossing of the north-south Cardo and east-west Decumanus is on a slight hill, now known as the Plaça Sant

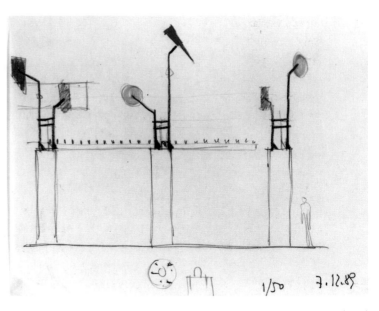

Hotel entrance porch, Puerto Vallarta, Mexico (1988)

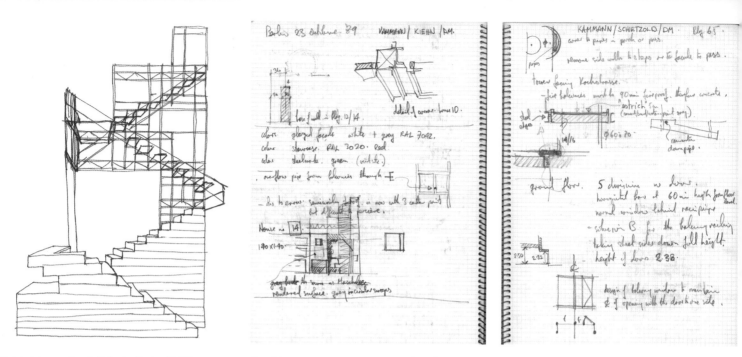

Hotel staircase, Puerto Vallarta, Mexico (1988)

Site visit notebook, Kochstraße, Berlin (1989)

Jaume. Here the two political powers, the Catalan Government and the Town Hall, face each other in their respective palaces where the Forum used to be. Curiously the streets are tilted 45°, similar to the 19th century grid of Idelfons Cerdà.

Between the wider grid, within the Roman walls, rings of closer, narrow streets allowed the first layer of density in the inward growing city. New settlements and villas lay beyond its walls until the 13th century, when a further wall was built to protect them. This contained a flood plain to the west, a neighbourhood called the Raval, referring to population living beyond the walls.

The main streets within the second walls have the marked radial structure of the original trade routes to the four original gates of the Roman foundation. Beyond the Rondas that follow the route of the medieval walls we have the 19th century grid which absorbed former settlements like Gracia and Sants. Now the city has a metropolitan size, between the sea and the mountains and the two river valleys of the Llobregat and Besos. As usual, political recognition is slow to recognise the geographical reality of the city today that needs a metropolitan administration.

The purpose of this very brief summary of how to read the streets of Barcelona is to point out how easy it is to understand. This is one reason why so many schools of architecture visit the city from the four corners of the world. It is easy to explain and easy to read its historical development.

In the fast expansion of Barcelona in the 1960s buildings went up before the streets. It was not until democracy returned, twenty years later, that this was solved with streets, squares, parks and the new Rondas (this time a friendly urban motorway "ring"). These were designed by engineers, together with architects, in preparation for the 1992 Olympics and after. The players worked together as a team, led by their Mayor and supported by the great majority of citizens.

After the buildings without streets and the series of individual high blocks of flats, the city of Barcelona began a decade of "repairing" the damage and neglect. This was like Berlin after the careless rebuilding, following the virus of Central Business Districts (CBD), that preferred single tall buildings set in a car park, reached by a motorway. All this was imported from the USA. Well, the USA has so much virgin territory that they can almost afford to extend forever into the green suburbs and leave the centres to rot. Europe, as the Dutch know well, treasures its land.

Barcelona also suffered from the streetless virus, which still crops up today with buildings that do their best to ignore the street. Architectural magazines seem to love such structures, together with the top architects and their top clients. That's why I always insist on the traditional value of the corridor street, its corners and the timely square, pocket garden and say, every 500m, a notable piece of architecture. It is all part of the appropriate architectural form of the city: its grammar.

Cities Sometimes Shrink

"The other part of me wanted to get out and stay out, but this was the part I never listened to. Because if I ever had I would have stayed in the town where I was born – I might even have got rich – small town rich, an eight-room house, two cars in the garage, chicken every Sunday, and the Reader's Digest on the living-room table, the wife with a cast-iron permanent and me with a brain like a sack of Portland cement. You take it, friend. I will take the big, sordid, dirty, crooked city." (Raymond Chandler).

I found this quotation in the architectural historian Mark Girouard's *Cities and People*, and could not resist repeating it. Like Chandler's hero, I like what I call dirty gritty cities that have bustle and activity. The roar with a sudden silence, the energy and then the charm of street cafes. Cities that suffer and celebrate, shoulder to shoulder. That's Glasgow, Liverpool and Barcelona for me. The great metropolitan cities of the world are aloof with global power. Somewhat grander in their public façades of places and buildings. But who can deny their special attraction, London, Paris, New York…

We are informed that, soon, three-quarters of the world's population will have moved from the country into cities. Not only the character in the quotation from Raymond Chandler, but those attracted to find work, moving from where there is none. From the third, fourth and fifth worlds, that we in the city know little of, they come crowding in, offering cheap labour, welcomed by some, rejected by others who feel threatened.

The city gains different cultures and cheaper labour. The drawback is that the city economy has its rhythms of prosperity and recession. Downturns arrive on maybe a ten year cycle, the result always of over production, combined with a miscalculated confidence when prospects appear too good and the future bright.

Exploding cities are like exploding businesses, a rapid increase in work means an expanding structure, difficult to reduce when the work is no longer there. Cities should only expand with care which can only come through a meditated political decision. It is obviously not just a question of available land, which the building industry is happy to have, taking profits from increasing land values, the bounty for that sector. For the public authority there is the question of transport, education, and health care, apart from other facilities like libraries and recreation. Expansion has to be related to density to avoid running costs, it also implies adding new administrative identities and local government. Such significant change cannot be left in the hands of the private sector.

During the greater part of the 20th century, functional planning came into fashion, although it took a long time to develop, discuss and approve. The problem was that it defined the future use of land, together with major road systems, all of which froze development requirements, impossible to guess, set against the changing lifestyles of citizens in the future. On top of this town and country planning failed to deal with form and instead kept to defined, supposedly logical, densities and use. But were they really logical?

Giving form to an idea is what architecture is all about. Normally a town plan is considered valid for a generation which means twenty years, and is then available for revision. This has proved a trap. The reality of cities is that they are a constant flux of ideas, unexpected investment opportunities and changing cultural values. The answer probably lies with a broad strategic plan for the city that should be a mainly written document with purely indicative images to clarify the intentions of the text. This provides an overall framework which identifies problems to be solved and opportunities. The project, or plan, comes later, when it can be carried out immediately.

In Barcelona the Olympics provided the opportunity to open the city to the sea, to house the Olympic Village and Port. This provided a stepping stone to the strategy of adjusting the city to the former industrial lands to the East. This fulfilled the 19th century proposal that the great Diagonal avenue should be extended to the sea, creating a new business district and another harbour. The second step would be to grow a new business area, based on creative industries, known as 22@. Since there is seldom the finance or the means of doing everything at once, a political decision is necessary to determine priorities. Which comes first? In this case, of course, it was the Olympic Village and Port.

Once approved politically and explained to the public, the professionals can get to work on a project –not a plan— to be carried out immediately. It is a fusion of the project with the plan. The project is about the architecture of the city, its connecting streets, the forms of the buildings that define its spaces, the frequency of punctuation with different kinds of spaces. This is all about applying the lessons of the architectural grammar of the historical European city to incorporate social

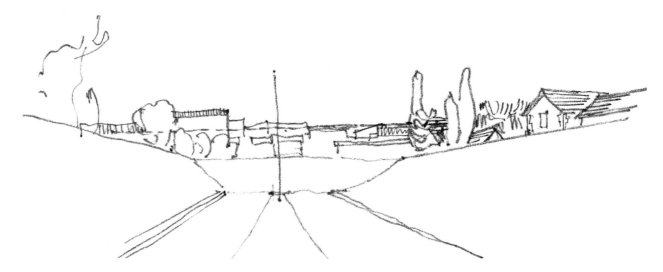

Avenue approach to the bridge (sketchbook), Aix en Provence, France (1990)

and technical circumstances which relate to the additional demands of a growing population.

Cities are mankind's greatest work of art. Art does not come from a committee. There must be an author, or usually authors, for every project. The authorship of buildings includes both public and private clients.

Cities don't only expand into fresh territory. They can also fill the gaps that are always appearing within the existing urban scene. Disused factories and railway lines are a typical example.

Citizens should be aware of how much his or her built environment influences behaviour or mental stress. It is here all the time. You cannot simply choose it or reject it like a book, a film, a play or an exhibition. You are obliged to live within the architecture that surrounds you. It is an important part of your life, so it needs looking after. It is there: the hidden city waiting to be rediscovered and cared for.

There was a moment in Barcelona, an election time, when different political parties defended or attacked urban design questions, basically aesthetic ones, like in favour of paved squares or in favour of pocket gardens. One example was to be for or against two diagonal walls designed by the sculptor Richard Serra that divided an open space to separate young children playing, with their mothers sitting watching, from hefty adolescents kicking a ball about.

How often do political parties get involved in both aesthetic and pragmatic questions of how the city should respond? We should wish that our elected representatives were more sensitive to the importance of the form of the village, town or city for the benefit of all ages. This should be part of their political programme.

Coming back to the question of what is the ideal size of a city even democracy has its territorial limits. If too small it is unable to supply all the needs of its citizens and is likely to be open to the interests of a minority in power. If too large those at the perimeter feel unrepresented, being too far from the centre. So when a city expands its political structure should be adjusted to its new territorial reality. If it doesn't, then democracy will be in danger of breaking down at the edge. The city will be confronted with social and physical problems that have escaped its notice and become difficult to repair.

View of the centre after the bridge (sketchbook), Aix en Provence, France (1990)

We should refer to repairing cities, rather than planning. Idiotic proposals for the city of the future occasionally appear in the press. The imagery is usually from a comic, or a rather infantile proposal, exploiting the untold marvels of technology. The city's life is larger than ours and should be treated with more respect.

The historical city contains many lessons for the present. All that is needed is a little observation, sitting on a bench or in a street café to watch how the city flows by. How citizens use their city tells us a great deal about how it really works or doesn't. Our former Mayor, Pasqual Maragall, used to leave his family for a few days now and again and live with neighbours in different districts to get to know them and their dreams. His is an example for all those with political responsibility, not to live apart from reality.

There is a lot of companionship in a city but there is also a great deal of loneliness. Perhaps we have too much respect for each other's privacy. That is understandable. However just saying "hello", with a smile, to the man or woman sweeping the street makes both of us feel a little better, and brings us closer to the family of man. The early Liverpool life of the Beatles allowed them to create many of their social songs and music.

Cities grow and need repairing. Now and again in history we learn that some cities shrink. Industry closes and the workers migrate. The United States city of Detroit has lost more than 60% of its population, resulting in something like 800,000 buildings empty or demolished. It depended on the automobile industry alone. A similar fate befell many of the coal mining towns of Europe and left generations in the abyss of unemployment.

We were once asked, for an exhibition, to provide an idea for a large area of urban land once occupied by an important industrial complex. The city was Turin. Examining early maps of the area we realised how it used to be, with agriculture and pastures. This gave us the idea that the site was large enough for an urban farm.

Many elderly people, retired too early following the closure of the factories, had nothing much to do. Our suggestion was to provide a farming institute where people could learn to manage allotments on a grand scale and how to produce dairy products from the cows in the urban fields. After a time the hides could be used as leather for a number of products. We enjoyed the challenge, but it remains unrealised, only a utopian idea.

There is another more tragic aspect of cities. Their buildings and citizens can become targets of war in a horrific way. In the moment of writing tens of thousands of citizens are being killed and wounded by shelling and bombing in Syria. Not far away the people of Gaza are being submitted to deadly technology, activated by just pressing digital buttons. The killer is unseen and unknown. He or she has no sense of killing, manipulating an abstract digital instrument. This destruction continues not only in Gaza, but in Afghanistan and Pakistan too.

When power was transferred from cities to nations, with questionable frontiers, the risk of conflict was increased. It is not that cities are havens of peace, but the likelihood of conflict is at a different scale.

Is it time to reconsider returning to a world of city states rather than nations? Trade and culture, production and distribution, people and knowledge, flow from city to city. Cities are communicating constantly, forming economic city regions that cross what are now artificial frontiers of nations. Perhaps in reality national boundaries no longer exist in Europe and other world mega communities.

The kings and queens, generals and feudal lords, the power of nation, or state, is frequently unrelated to the economic and social power of the city. If this is true it places the geographical and man-made frontiers of power in need of

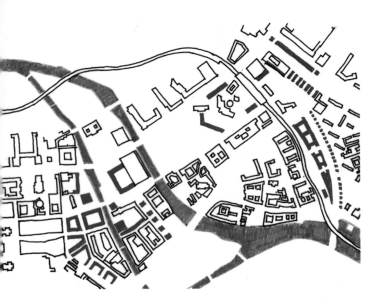

Stadtforum – Ideas for Berlin, Old Centre, Berlin (1991)

Stadtforum – Ideas for Berlin, Alexanderplatz, Berlin (1991)

a structural revision. This should grow outwards and upwards, from the cities and not downwards from the present bastions of national power and the dictat of a superseded democracy.

This is a complex vision and one requiring study and debate. This notion is not utopian. It draws upon the history of cities and their citizens. Meanwhile a submerged conflict is perpetuated, well worth bringing to the surface for debate and perhaps to precipitate change.

The Modern Movement Now

It was a delicate moment, a young reporter, from the BBC, wished to interview the architect of an unfinished building that was a popular landmark in the city. She was accompanied by a local architect who was a personal friend of the architect she was coming to meet, but was critical of the project.

It was a building that suffered from being massively over ambitious in time and scale, like the city itself, full of stops and starts, while values changed from generation to generation. The architect the BBC reporter was going to meet was the fourth generation to work on the yet unfinished building, himself approaching retirement. The architect with her had once worked for the architect they had come to interview. He was familiar with both sides of opinion about the continuation of the project. Until now he had not seen the inside of the finished nave.

When they arrived at the gate the architect, Jordi Bonet, was waiting for them. He stood against the backcloth of the soaring façade of the Passion of Christ, now dotted about with figures by the sculptor Subirachs. The sculptor had spent half his life on the building, illustrating episodes from the Bible. His work shocking to many of the faithful.

The three entered the Basilica of the *Sagrada Família*. The five naves, with their forest of treelike columns reaching up to the filtered light from the heavens, were all to the scale of Brobdingnag. The space was filled with tourists from Lilliput,

Urban design for Rummelsburger Bucht, Berlin (1992)

wandering, lost in thought, within this spectacular romantic stage of awe and terror, a distant relation to religion.

The enthusiasm of the old architect captivated the two visitors. The constructor's elevator, trembled up through the voids over the naves, to reach the temporary platforms from where the future central tower will one day rise over the strange, compressed, building. It was an after-Gaudí event, with natural stone shuttering encasing the reinforced concrete of the structure to comply with present day building regulations, saying goodbye to Gaudí's ambition to use the supreme compressive strength of stone.

Is this building a parody of the original project? Or does it express an architectural journey through time, with various styles in apparent confusion?

When the two visitors finally found themselves back on the pavements of the city they were left-thinking, trying to puzzle it all out. Perhaps that's why two million people visit it every year, much to the annoyance of the neighbours who have an ambiguous relationship to this monument. It is odd because it has no real function, churches are losing their clients, cathedrals are not in demand.

The BBC reporter was just amazed. You can be sure that her listeners appreciated the curiosity of the building, more like a fairy tale than just another Walt Disney attraction for the tourists. It is a strange building and somehow relates to the tale of the Modern Movement of Architecture, not in its style. It is neither modern nor old. The space within is not logical but it is symbolic. Above all perhaps it is puzzling and sensual. Gaudí did better with his earlier work with many valid lessons for the Modern Movement in architecture.

So what is the Modern Movement in architecture? If architects themselves are not clear of the difference between Modern Architecture and the Modern Movement in architecture it is hardly surprising that the "man in the street" is even more confused. Occasional articles in the newspapers and magazines tend to follow what is sometimes called the "wow" factor in new architecture, highlighting what surprises us most. There is almost reverential attention to architects whose work is emotional, rather than following a critical, rational route.

The Modern Movement explains how, over a long period, certain factors have prevailed. It has involved the incorporation of human and social objectives. Architects were no longer only designing for the powerful. As a result the best architecture can be found in housing, but is also expressed in the pedagogical spatial relationships in education, health care, workplaces and in the architecture of cities.

This revolution has also involved the transfer of craft to industrial design. New, mass produced, designed objects include everything from domestic utensils and furniture to factory produced building components and the beauty of vehicles for road, sea or air travel.

Historians, critics and writers, as well as architects, have doubts about just when the Modern Movement in architecture began. Intellectually it begins with the end of the medieval period when the religious "status quo" was questioned. Cultural rebirth was stimulated with renewed appreciation of Greek and Roman architecture. The importance of mankind at the centre of creation was illustrated by the geometrical proportions of the human body within both a square and circle. The supremacy of God was replaced by the reciprocal relationship of humanity.

The modern world began there. However the fundamental shift came when the classical gave way to the wider knowledge collected in the *Encyclopédie ou Dictionnaire Raisonné des Sciences, des Arts et des Métiers* (1751-72) edited by Denis Diderot and Jean le Rond d'Alembert, which changed the way people thought.

When the roots of classical architecture began to be questioned, some architects turned back to the medieval for inspiration. This coincided with the study of the medieval archives which supported growing architectural interest in their approach to a clear resolution of structure and space. This was accompanied with a renewed discipline of decoration that included abstract forms related to Islamic and Oriental cultures. There was also an outbreak of critical ideals, supporting a Gothic revival. So there begun not only a battle of styles but also a battle of ideals. This enriched the aspect of the Modern Movement as it led to an enquiry towards the future, even if it led to an open choice for architects who turned to different styles for different uses, under the guise of Romanticism.

Emerging from this eclectic panorama we find the rational geometry and mathematics of engineers and science including community health emerging from the industrial revolution. The Arts and Crafts movement emerged from the simplicity of traditional craftsmanship, with inspiration from nature itself. All this allowed historians to prefer situating the pioneers of the Modern Movement around the mid nineteenth century.

Both periods, one from the Renaissance and the other from the emerging social awareness, are focussed in the words and works of William Morris: "I do not want art for a few, any more than education for a few, or freedom for a few". His question "What business have we with art at all unless all can share it?" introduces us to the twentieth century.

This is the moment when we should briefly go back to look at the time-line of the Modern Movement in architecture beginning with the Renaissance.

The architecture of the Renaissance can be recognised by the composition of façades into base, column and entablature, both for the whole façade and for the details around the openings. These buildings are best observed through a contemplation of the proportions of their modular system, mainly because their discipline demands more intellectual effort than emotional.

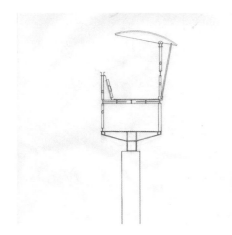

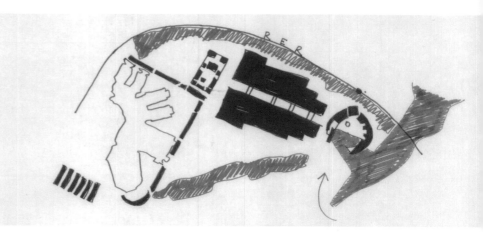

'Mistral' footbridge, Aix en Provence, France (1993)   Trade Exhibition Halls urban design, Villepinte, Paris, France (1993)

The humanism of the Renaissance can be found, but not always, in the reference of its proportions to the human body. The archetype is the well-known figure of a man with outstretched arms and legs within a perfect square and circle by Leonardo da Vinci and others. This can be observed by seeing that the root of the penis is at half the height of a man and is the centre of the square while the umbilicus, or "belly button", is the centre of the circle. Compositions based on the square and the length of its diagonals from corner to corner created what was called the golden section, which was used to determine the scale and location of many of the openings in walls.

That the human body might serve as the basis of a sublime proportion broke the aesthetic allegiance to the dictatorship of theology. This released a new creative energy that could emerge from critical observations. It was this freedom to doubt that allowed a critical discussion. It was this that foreshadowed the Modern Movement, focussed upon the architecture of buildings and cities.

This implies that the early Renaissance was a question of a personal expression of a classical vocabulary. This tendency distinguished the work of different architects, from Brunelleschi (the dome of Florence cathedral), through Michelangelo (the *Biblioteca Laurenziana* in Florence) to Andrea Palladio (*Villa Rotonda*, Vicenza).

Critics and historians are inclined to tag a name onto different periods of time to identify cultural movements when certain aspects dominate. The suffixism, that denotes a doctrine, theory or system, sits uncomfortably on the complex creative side of culture. The thread of these –isms runs through long sequences of times, occasionally with a faint re-appearance within another ism. On the other hand, the expression of revolt is referred to as the "avant-guard".

This undulating swell of different currents, up one moment, down the next, in fashion and styles can create the shock of the new. In reality these sudden changes are often caused by explosive social events that provoke a time for a revolutionary response, heralding a new, or renewed, –ism. This is what we should bear in mind if we are to understand and accept the concept of the long period of the Modern Movement in architecture from the Renaissance to our own times. The right to doubt and criticise is fundamental, together with the gradual swing from architecture for the powerful to architecture for the people.

The road forward was provided by a softening of the geometrical discipline of the early Renaissance. Expanding

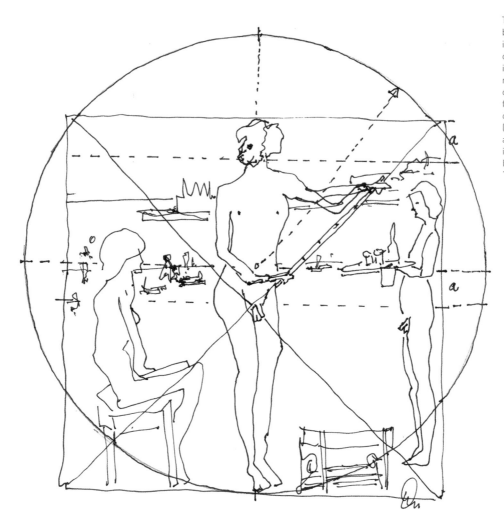

The Lines of Beauty by Leonardo da Vinci illustrated the humanism of the Renaissance. This illustration, invites a reflection that beauty in our own days also can be found in the proportions of our human relationships. (The sketch was drawn after fragments of illustrations by Aubrey Beardsley for the Play "Salome" by Oscar Wilde).

skills of perspective introduced an increasing interest in movement through space in architecture. This can be observed with the itinerary of entering a building, including its setting, either in the city or within the landscape. Staircases continue this progression. Eventually the Baroque style spreads movement to the façade surface and its decoration.

We can assume this is part of the growing trend towards a peak in the Romantic expression of a "way of feeling". Baudelaire, the French nineteenth century poet, is said to have interpreted the word "modernité" as a fleeting ephemeral experience of life in an urban metropolis. We can understand this as a more humanist gesture towards a more sensual architecture.

The Romantic mantle was spread widely over all the creative arts, from literature, Byron and Walter Scott for example, music, Beethoven and Chopin and the thundering operas of Wagner, to painting, Caspar David Friedrich, especially with his *Cross in the Mountains*. This reflects the awe and mysterious attraction to the danger and challenge of mountains which had to be crossed in the pilgrimage of writers and artists to reach the ruins of Roman architecture. Roman of course being the very root of the word 'Romantic' itself.

The war of words between the Romantics of the Gothic Revival and the Neo-Classicists was often due to the claims that each was doing both, or one claiming to be the other.

In England we find examples of Gothic fantasies in cottages and rural homes, together with artificial ruins and grottoes dotted around the great landscape gardens of country houses. Capability Brown, one of many who created "informal" English landscapes and gardens wove such artifice into his contrived natural landscape at Stourhead. However the most famous must be the royal residence of Windsor Castle, renovated and rebuilt in the 18th century and later.

Barcelona has more recent examples of Neo-Romantic architecture with the fantasy bridge over the Carrer del Bisbe, linking two buildings of the *Generalitat* by Rubió I Bellver (1923) and *Bellesguard House* by Gaudí (1902) built on the ruins of the Palace of King Martí. There is a third example in Ricard Bofill's *Walden 7*, a vertical village in Sant Just Desvern (1970-75) close to Barcelona. The continuation, after Gaudí, of the *Sagrada Família* should also be considered a romantic enterprise.

A full Romantic style is difficult to find in architecture without an attendant adjective. It is often there, either with a touch of humanism or the magical wand of the irrational.

Till now we have traced the thread of the Modern Movement in architecture mainly through buildings, together with a passing reference to the architecture of the landscape. It is now important to cast a glance towards the architecture of the city and urban settlements from the Renaissance onwards.

I will begin just at the start of the Renaissance focus on the voids created by the streets, their crossings and meeting places, with my own personal discovery of where it all began.

It was a lesson in the understanding of the geography and history of a certain space before converting it into a public place.

The story began in Sienna around 1988. We entered a competition, which we won. The brief was to repair the area between the *Piazza Matteotti* and *Piazza Grimsci* on the way down to the famous *Piazza del Campo*. Duccio Malagamba, an architect from our office, now a well-known international photographer, was with me. When we were about to leave, talking together, he realised I had never been to the little town of Pienza. So we took the country roads through the marvellous Toscana countryside till we approached the silhouette of a row of buildings running along a ridge for about a kilometre. In the centre one could pick out a cluster of large buildings, including a church that advanced over a cliff.

Duccio explained to me that this was the birthplace of Bartolomeo Piccolomini who became Pope Pius II. Brought up in the cultural home of a family with strong humanist convictions, he chose his hometown to establish the Papal residence for the summer. That was in 1458. We approached the centre through a suburb to find the high street that ran along the ridge through the old town. We stopped the car and walked to the main point just where the high street kinked to the left, following the ridge. The physical incident was an obvious space to create a place.

The cathedral was to be arranged along the main axis, which coincided with the bisection of the angle that marked the bend in the high street. This was to be accompanied by two palaces, his own, the *Palazzo Piccolomini*, lining up with the angle of the high street we had just driven up, and the *Palazzo Borgia*, for his cardinals, on the left side, lining up with the other arm of the high street. This arrangement created a trapezium shape, placed in front of the cathedral.

Opposite the cathedral, on the other side of the old high street, the Pope arranged for the *Town Hall* to be built,

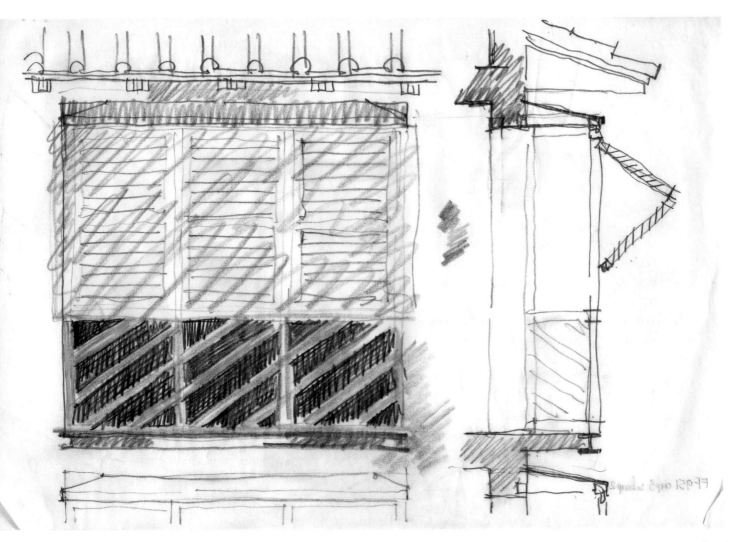

Detail of bay window and screen, Florence, Italy (1994)

completing the composition. The Pope apparently followed the construction closely with the help of a Florentine architect Bernardo Rossellino who had previously worked with Leon Alberti, a humanist and the major theorist of the Renaissance.

Piccolomini's childhood memories of his little town allowed him to interpret both the topography and the history of the place. He was able to comprehend the significance of both with such skill that his townscape appears natural and timeless to the visitor.

Geography and history, especially when you can feel it by not only seeing where it happened, but also understanding it through personal observation which architecture allows you, helps you to understand the present. Perhaps the Pope invested more than he should have done, in the place of his childhood. He challenged the world to raise the professional level of the architecture of the city.

Just as architects tired of the modules and other rules of the Renaissance, so they tired of its planning. First, the grandeur of the Baroque. This is best illustrated by Paris. The first steps include the residence of *Vaux le Vicomte*, near the city itself. The house was built in the middle of the 17th century with extraordinary gardens designed by André Le Nôtre, the principal gardener of the King Louis XIV of France, who later designed the park of Versailles. I once walked the gardens of *Vaux* until brought to a stop by a wide canal at least one kilometre long. It cut across the visual axis, half-way before it continued into the forest. I realised that these gardens were designed to be contemplated from the palace and were not for use: a demonstration of wealth and power.

In a way the power of the Baroque city plan (and landscape) was to impose the artificial conquest over nature. This was far from the concept of the gentle adaptation to nature of English parks.

The need to impose the artificial was adopted by organisations, military or civil. The grid plan is as old as cities,

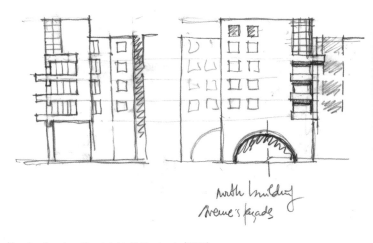

Housing façades, Maastricht, Netherlands (1994)

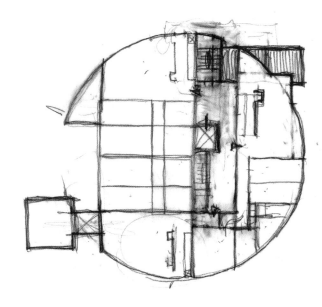

Circular housing plan, Maastricht, Netherlands (1994)

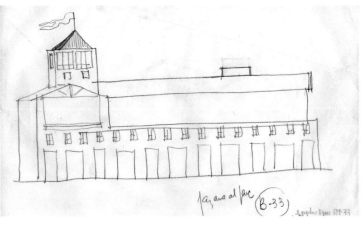

Civic centre for urban renovation, Florence, Italy (1994)

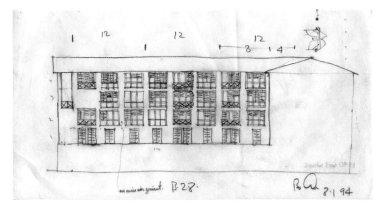

Housing for urban renovation, Florence, Italy (1994)

Deep down everyone in one moment or other is an architect, moving furniture to create a place. In the Italian hill town of Pienza, that was the home town of Bartolomeo Piccolomini when he became both Pope and Architect he arranged the buildings, like furniture, to create a place.

in stark contrast to plans that grew up organically through the meeting of trade routes or through settling on hilltops, for defence.

The industrial revolution slipped in almost unnoticed between the 18th and 19th century. The poor were there already but spread out and generally accepting their place in the upstairs and downstairs of society. The production of coal and iron and their application to heavy industry, and the necessity to establish lines of transportation, gathered the poor together around mines, factories, railways and shipping.

The recent French Revolution and the Napoleonic Wars which followed provided an unsettling background to the industrial revolution. Incidentally, an agricultural revolution was also required to meet the demands of a rising population. The slavery of child labour replaced the slavery of captured Africans, while a rising middle class amassed unexpected wealth, seeking the advantages of the established landed gentry.

The new industries gathered the workers together around existing towns and cities to be near work 24 hours, day and night. Their accommodation was rudimentary, back to back houses laid out in row after row, with neither cross ventilation, nor proper sanitation. Families slept three or four to a bed, often all in one room. The poor, when dispersed across the countryside, had no choice but to accept their situation. Once crowded together they shared their brutal circumstances. Soon they became restless and now and again assembled to protest and occasionally to riot.

This occurred throughout Europe creating the "slums" in every industrial city and along the valleys where the mills were established. Apart from the explosive social situation, the city itself was creating unsanitary ghettos that threatened to spread disease. All this must be set side by side with the rising quality of life enabled by the products of the industrial revolution.

Charles Dickens observed this social contrast between the middle class and workers, or "hands" in his novel *Hard Times* (1854). The book was written to incite thought and help mould attitudes to burning problems when Britain changed over from a rural to an urban civilisation inside two generations. It is worth quoting Dickens to understand how trapped and bewildered a person could be, reduced to the value of his hands. He would be fined if he spoke to fellow workers. Conditions of living were intolerable, damaging to physical and psychological well-being. The rich and poor, employers and working people, lived at such different standards that they were inevitably arrayed against each other in class struggle.

"In the hardest working part of Coketown, in the innermost fortifications of that ugly citadel, where Nature was as strongly bricked out as killing airs and gases were bricked in; at the heart of the labyrinth of narrow courts upon courts, and close streets upon streets, which had come into existence piecemeal, every piece in a violent hurry for some one man's purpose, and the whole an unnatural family, shouldering, and trampling, and pressing one another to death;... a race who would have found more favour with some people, if Providence had seen fit to make them only hands, or, like the lower creatures of the sea-shore, only hands and stomachs –lived a certain Stephen Blackpool, fourty years age".

Dickens' dramatic images can be compared to Shakespeare's tragedies.

A decade before *Hard Times* Dickens's friend Friedrich Engels wrote *The Condition of the Working Class in England*, which led to his co-authorship, with Karl Marx, of the *Communist Manifiesto* in 1848.

At the end of February 2013, under the title *Down and Out* in the weekly *New Statesman* (London), the journalist Nicholas Lezard wrote:

"Money has its own gravity: when it disappears, it takes everything with it, and scrimping and saving just does not seem to have any effect".

Dickens, today, surely would put his pen to paper for this reverse problem. Instead of too much work there is none at all, too many are in a cage again, with politicians in a class apart. Already the clean iconic towers, demonstrating the wealth and power of the Financial Market, are destroying not only the individual character of cities but people as well.

Let's now look and see how the Modern Movement in architecture handled the situation in the 19th and 20th centuries.

The Modern Movement in Barcelona was sealed by the Catalan civil engineer Ildefons Cerdà who started things off with his topological plan of Barcelona and its surroundings produced in 1855. This provided the information necessary for any extension of the city. A city that had been confined to its medieval limits until the pressures, of the Industrial Revolution, which arrived late in Catalonia. The intolerable asphyxia of its citizens caused by its tight streets, high and dense buildings and workshops, with a density of 859 inhabitants per hectare, finally led to permission to tear down the military walls in 1854.

After completing his geographical survey, Cerdà went on to produce a social survey of Barcelona, *Monografía de la clase obrera de Barcelona en 1856*. He not only studied groups according to incomes and living expenses but also the dwellings and streets. For example, in housing he found that the rich enjoyed 21 m² per person while craftsmen were limited to 12 m² and labourers to 8 m². He also, perhaps surprisingly,

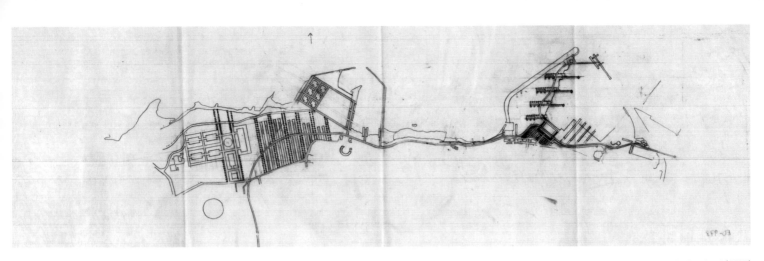

Waterfront urban design, Edinburgh, Scotland (1995)

discovered that the poor paid a higher rent for their square metre than the rich for theirs.

This direct contact with the reality of urban conditions through Cerda's pioneer field-study obviously tempered his political attitudes. His understanding of these urban conditions, formulated later in the theoretical work *Teoría General de la Urbanización* (1867) led him to consider communications, density, housing conditions, social and neighbourhood grouping, together with social and other public services of fundamental importance.

The original plan was abused by speculation. In the 1980s efforts were made to restore it with the idea of public gardens in the middle of each island. It is better to explore and discover the gardens now and again when you walk along the tree-lined streets with their cut-off corners (allowing steam trams to turn, and space for loading and unloading, but awkward for pedestrians). It is also important to notice that the democratic grid is tilted to a NW/SE axis to obtain sun on all four façades of the urban block, curiously on the same axis used by the Romans when they founded the city.

The Modern Movement was not only rational but also sought for functional simplicity. This was best explained by one of the most influential thinkers of the period at the end of the 19th century. William Morris was a poet and the greatest artist-craftsman of his times. He called for a return to functional simplicity in "the arts of life" and reference to history. He researched the past, "not to imitate it or to repeat it, but to study it wisely, and to be taught by it". He is usually recognised as one of the greatest designers of all times: his furniture, wallpaper and fabrics are still available today.

Morris' leadership in promoting Arts and Crafts was an important contribution to the simple and direct expression of the use of the object, sweeping away all that was unnecessary. I visited his own home, the *Red House* (1858) at Bexleyheath in Kent in 1961 to understand its contribution to the Modern Movement. His architect was his friend Philip Webb. Together they combined a disciplined domestic historical tradition with a spatial distribution, responding to the expected creative social life that could change the future.

Morris was only 24. His home's enclosing bricks of beautiful red exposed its honest construction. Its sturdy L-shaped plan is like a fragment from his Oxford University monastic quadrangle. The memories hang in the air of reading aloud Ruskin's *The Seven Lamps of Architecture*. This reference,

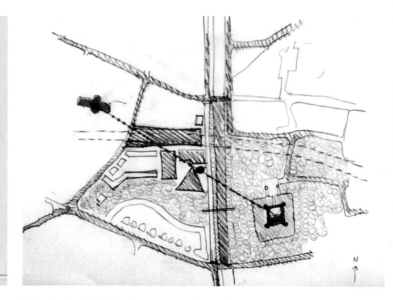

Ideas for Battersea Park, London, England (1995)

Urban design, City Hall and centre related to castle and church, Helmond, Netherlands (1995)

together with a red brick well and its steeple-like conical roof, somehow defined the outside space and its binding relationship to the landscape of the apple orchard. As I walked around the building I noticed that the windows of all the main rooms faced away from the sun.

The architect, who showed us around, explained that the house was designed during an extremely hot summer. William Morris was unable to accept heat and insisted that the corridors should be placed around the Southern walls to isolate the main rooms. However the architect added that Morris was also concerned that his projected frescoes and fabrics should be properly protected.

The interior decoration, walls, ceilings, stairs, doors and furniture are all designed with sublime craftsmanship with reference to the romance of the Gothic. There is also an uncanny future reference to C.R. Mackintosh and others who came after him. The German critic, Hermann Muthesius, described the *Red House* as "the first to be conceived and built

as a unified whole, inside and out, the very first example in the history of the modern house".

William Morris was not only sensitive to culture and social concerns, but also to the importance of architecture and its environment, promoting the Society for the Protection of Ancient Buildings.

In Vienna, the architect Adolf Loos, famous for his 1908 essay *Ornament and Crime* in which he stated "The evolution of culture marches with the elimination of ornament from useful objects". His *Casa Loos* (1910) in Michaelerplatz, Vienna, was an example of a fenestration with the elimination of decoration of a series of simple square windows. The flower boxes were added by an embarrassed City Council. On a previous trip to England he recognised the simplicity of the domestic architecture of the Arts and Crafts movement. Morris's ideas were filtering through to the Modern Movement.

In Barcelona, Eugeni d'Ors began writing his "Glossari" (comments), a series published in "La Veu de Catalunya" between 1906 and 1917. He introduced the term "Noucentisme" (meaning both the nineteenth century and the new century) implying a cultural change from a fading Modernism. As a philosopher he supported the value of the concept of arbitrary choice, a voluntary decision, in this case to define a cultural identity of Catalonia. This was a turn towards the natural heritage of the classical Mediterranean country, for an ordered institutional country, a structure that could support the diversity of the modern age. Different, only in the roots of a style: Gothic for Morris; Classical for Eugeni d'Ors.

Art Nouveau was a soft-Baroque child of the Arts and Crafts, as was Modernism in Catalonia. They were also cousins of the Garden City movement that included utopian villages with good intentions.

Unfortunately, after the Great War of 1914-1918, now referred to as the First World War, European governments were keen to cover the barbarity of generals on all sides. They set up campaigns like "homes for heroes", allowing developers to build suburb after suburb that had little to do with the ideals of the Garden City.

The Deutsche Werkbund was founded in Munich in 1907 to reform the German Arts and Crafts through a genuine rapprochement between artists and producers. Although several well-known pioneers of modern architecture were associated with the Werkbund, it is recognised more for its hot debates between progressives and conservatives over its objectives. This produced a schism after the First World War, when Walter Gropius set up the progressive alternative known as the Bauhaus, an important experiment in design education that lasted for fourteen years until it was suppressed by the Nazis in 1933.

In 1965, Walter Gropius wrote to me that, when he travelled in Spain in 1907, "In Barcelona I met Puig I Cadafalch who showed me his ceramic collections and gave me a book *Rajoles Valencianes i Catalanes* by Josep Font I Gumà".

This letter came to me after I met him in Barcelona in 1961, when he was 78 years old. In conversation he explained that Puig i Cadafalch, architect, historian of medieval art and politician, invited him to a workshop (probably the former *1888 Restaurant* in the Ciutadella park) run by another architect, Antoni Gallissà. The boom in construction demand had made it imperative to introduce industrial production. Gropius told me that the visit impressed him, and helped him to understand the importance of industrial design.

So the Modern Movement in architecture runs through time. After the Medieval structures, surviving the Renaissance revolt, passing through the movement in space of the Baroque, onto the battle of the styles, leading to the simplicity of Arts and Crafts, via the Bauhaus and ultimately into our own times.

Meanwhile, in rapid succession, contemporary architectural historians have identified "styles" that have passed into common classifications like Expressionism, Constructivism (also de-Constructivism), Stark Rationalism, Art Deco, Industrial pre-Fabrication, Brutalism, Realism, post-Modernism, Hi-Tech, Smart Cities. Finally architecture lost its way in a round of iconic neo-Baroque digital towers and extravagant, computer generated forms. Perhaps the sting of the financial boom and collapse will allow a recovery of the true thread of the Modern Movement. Hopefully we will see a return to its constant humanist ingredients of rationalism, a touch of subtle romanticism and a focus on architecture's social and professional role. Only the uncertain future will decide.

and one man in his time plays many parts

Civic centre, Helmond, Netherlands (1995)

Housing, Java Eiland, Amsterdam, Netherlands (1995)

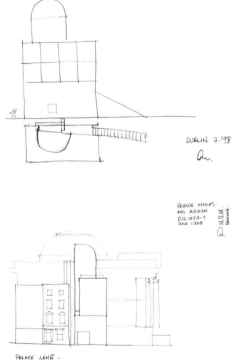

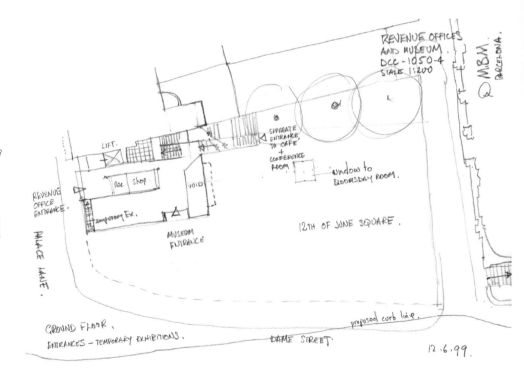

City square and office, Dame Street, Dublin, Ireland (1998)

Citizens First: Spaces for Minds and Body

The Ages of Man is a recurrent subject in history, from Greek mythology, through many different cultures. It has been used to structure poems, novels, and appears as a theme in all the arts. Sex, from youth to old age, was the subject of the curious collection of illustrations, gathered by Dr. George Witt and kept for a time, in the Secretum of the British Museum.

The opening lines of the "All the world's a stage" monologue from Shakespeare's *As You Like It* have been used to structure this book. In this context the stage is the architecture that wraps around our lives. Now it is time to look at the actors that make the city in the first place –the citizens themselves and their changing lives, independent and at the same time needing company, being dependent on others for their social and built environment.

Shakespeare uses Jacques in the play to introduce the word "lover" between the age of childhood and the age of the soldier. He adapts "lover" from the usual contemporary English meaning, "young adult", still in use in his time, instead of adolescent, a term introduced a century before to the English Court from the French. Love was the happiness that the young urban adults were seeking in the freedom of their outing in the Forest of Arden.

Shakespeare was 46 years old, when life expectancy was between 50 and 60 years for those who reached maturity. This vignette on the Ages of Man may explain not only his sense of lost youth but his irony towards the approach of Old Age. He retired twelve years later.

Shakespeare's seven ages of man's life are: 1) infancy, 2) childhood, 3) the lover, 4) soldier, 5) justice, 6) old age, and finally 7) extreme old age. Relating the seven ages to our built environment, the space around us, we could introduce an update to include an all-age city, town or village. This is vastly oversimplified:

1) infancy: spatial limitation (discovering the world around)
2) childhood: spatial discovery (beyond the house, experimentation and imagination, socially expanding)
3) the lover: need for space (discovering oneself and others with empathy and frustration)
4) the soldier: reality of space (courage to change the world)
5) justice: questioning space (concerns that there should be justice as it never catches up with reality)
6) old age: remembering space (wisdom and accepting its limits and doubts, or not)
7) extreme old age: loss of space (managing dependence).

Jan Gehl is an architect from Copenhagen, with an unusual empathy for citizens and their cities. He observes cities by walking along their streets and squares, crossing them and then sitting in cafés to open a conversation with a neighbour. His writing stresses the importance of human contacts, discussing the reason why many have moved to the city to live, to feel free, to exchange ideas, discover a wider knowledge, and pursue possible opportunities for work. I make sure that one of his early books, *Life Between Buildings*, is always close at hand. I had met Jan a few times when our paths have crossed at conferences.

When I met him for breakfast, we were served coffee, toast and eggs from an open kitchen across from a few wooden tables and chairs. Nearby, a cluster of sofas formed a living room space, all together, like one of Bristol's pocket squares. In this urban scene I found Jan already chatting with the friendly Polish staff.

We were in Bristol together to advise on an initiative for the Redcliffe Neighbourhood Development Forum. They had been working together with the local Architecture Centre, financed by the central government, Department of Culture spin-off, CABE (Commission for Architecture and the Built Environment). The object was to reduce a major traffic route that spurred off the local motorway system, splitting the community into two.

After two days of learning about the problem, walking through the area, in spite of the snow, listening to opinions, we arrived at the final afternoon for conclusions. Next to me I had Ben, an expert in movement. He was what we normally call a traffic engineer, but as he explained to me, traffic meant only cars and other vehicles, whereas movement included people. The influence of Gehl, after many years was widespread and spreading.

Ben's argument was that if we wanted to join the two separate communities then it was a question of narrowing the street and eliminating traffic lights. At first, I thought this too radical. I wanted to believe him but just could not quite get there. Then I reflected on my own observation that the average speed of a car in the centre of any city was roughly 12 km/hour (on the dash board). It was easy to see that nearly all drivers add 20 km/hour to all restricted speed limits, like 50 km/hour driving 70 km/hour to the next set of traffic lights, or when 30 km/hours driving at 50 km/hours. I began to understand his rational thinking.

Drivers will never really observe the speed limits, but still end up with an average of 12 km/hour. If the driver shares the same place as the pedestrian who walks between 4 km/hour and 5 km/hour –half the average speed of a car— then the street can handle safety concerns, if there is only one lane for traffic in each direction. The rest of the table were delighted that we had closed the gap between the split neighbourhood from about 80 to around 20m.

Then Ben Hamilton-Baille, to give his full name, came up with a blockbuster. He proposed that at the crossroads between the split neighbourhood there should be no traffic lights. This, he explained, goes to ensure that the driver of a vehicle, afraid of being hit on the crossing will go slowly to make sure he or she can pass safely. This brings his average speed to that of an ordinary person who is walking. The driver has lost the "advantage" of flying over the crossing as the light changes.

Now that pedestrian areas exist in many cities where at certain times cars are allowed, drivers are already adjusting their movements to those of the pedestrians. They still get to where they want to go. The proposal was radically exciting.

There still remains the danger of bicycles to pedestrians and the danger of traffic to cyclists. Cycle paths are difficult to manage in existing streets in the centre of a city. Cycles tend to wind their way between moving pedestrians. I have noticed that pedestrians, wilful creatures that they are, even step backwards sometimes, especially if they are window shopping. Ringing a bell can startle pedestrians too. A coloured cycle route helps, then cyclists can go faster. But pedestrians, often distracted, step onto the cycle route. In Berlin this is treated by the cyclist as a territorial invasion, who is inclined to insult the distracted pedestrian.

We have a neighbour who is confined to a wheelchair after being run over by a bicycle. There is a gap about education for movement in cities, towns and villages. Perhaps the network of the International Association of Educating Cities, founded at the first congress in Barcelona in 1990, will one day contribute to manage educating all movements.

Usually neighbourhood initiatives, with expert advice and given time, can reach the point of a reasonable proposition. Now the question was if the city authorities would carry the project forward. Could its construction be achieved within a reasonable time and not left on the table for another twenty years?

To close this political gap it will be necessary for the elected representatives of the city, and in particular its leader or leaders, to realise that they must assume the role of "city fathers" and be the real clients for the built environment. This should affect existing development and those proposed,

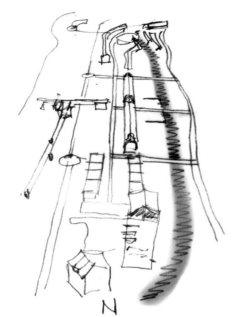

Railway station and holiday housing in the Pyrenees, Canfranc, Huesca, Aragon (2001)

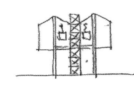

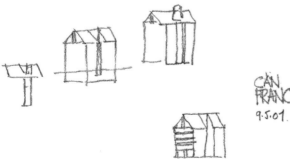

CAN FRANC. 9.5.01.

Hotel, Canfranc, Huesca, Aragon (2001)

rather than being lazy, leaving everything to the profit seeking developer-bank. This needs a cultural response to professional advice which is currently missing in too many European cities.

However there are many signs that this situation is being recognised to the benefit to the quality of life of the citizens. The first move would be that a strategic urban plan be considered as a written political document on the necessities of each district and an order of priorities. These documents should be produced by the elected Mayor and his advisors. This would then be the moment to commission a "project plan" sufficiently precise, defining the form of the built environment (public and private). This would establish the urban context of future buildings within and related to the public space which they define: the streets, squares, gardens and parks, as well as community services.

Although heights and street building lines will be rigid, a certain leeway should be allowed for the depth of the building, always within the limit of the density established for the area. This commission, because of its complexity, may well be best achieved through collaboration between external architects, working in tandem with the local city planning office. Form would then be added to the developing plan.

This system was used by ourselves in the design of the Olympic Village in Barcelona and worked well with the individual architects for the different buildings with whom we were able to discuss and adjust the architectural proposals. For the sake of the identity of the neighbourhood the façades were to be 80% the same material. In reality it turned out that one or two, well justified, exceptions were allowed.

What was important was the opportunity to have serious discussions between professionals. The density however had been defined by the city, by law. This is explained just as an example, but it does include two important proposals. The first is that the city must act as a proper client, not only by rules and regulations. The second key proposition is that town planners

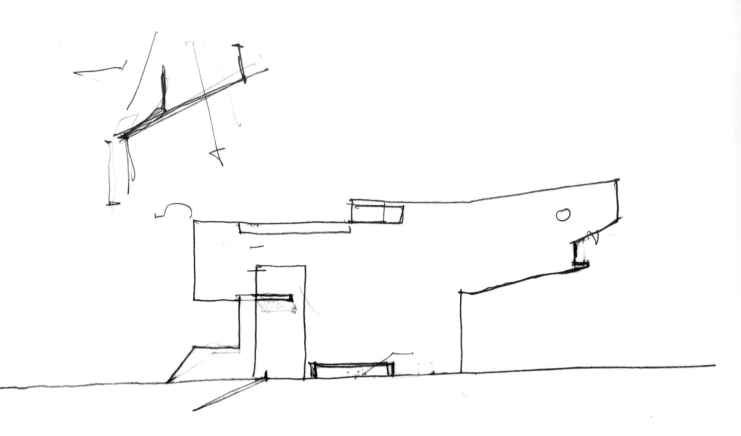

Design Hub Museum, Barcelona, Catalonia (2001)

are the most important collaborators with information and ideas. However the form of the built environment is a question of the architecture of the city.

Education: From Schools to City

"The first thing is to study your pupils more, for it is very certain that you do not know them", wrote Jean-Jacques Rousseau (1712-78) in the preface to his book *Émile ou de l'éducation*.

Education is like a minefield. If you wish to cross it every footstep is likely to explode in your face. If you interpret something it is bound to be thrown back with an alternative response which may seem reasonable. Often however it will be challenged enigmatically, with passion.

There are two major conflicts that never seem to die, from the Greeks to our own day. The first conflict is the class division between those who wish to lead the community, within a tight circle of those who have knowledge and the rest whom it is presumed will be more useful without knowledge. The Greek city-states existed on the division between citizens and slaves. The medieval period existed between those who knew about religious faith and those who had to be instructed. The second conflict is between the sexes, the male historically seen as superior. These two conflicts are still with us today.

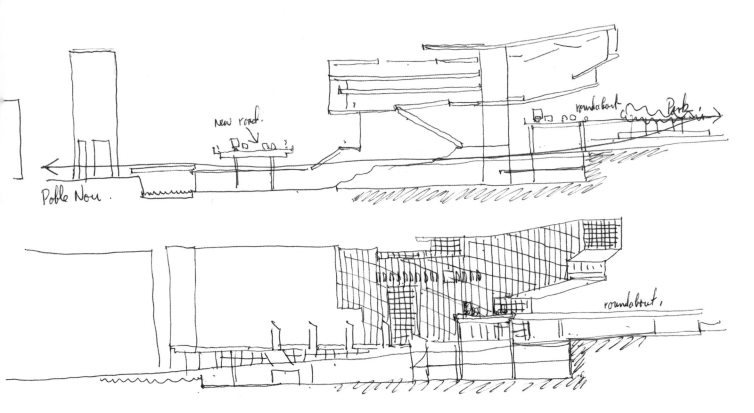

Design Hub Museum, Barcelona, Catalonia (2001)

Instruction or education, from a passionate point of view of absolutes, is a question about confidence, an emotional subject that leaves the question entangled, depending on whose side you are on. A question that lies in ambiguous territory. Only if one tries to move to a more civilised and reflexive point of view, a compromise in a conflictive situation would leave one to accept that education (drawing out the capacities of a child) does include instruction (guiding from past experience and established cultural behaviour). The first, education, is imaginative and experimental. The second, instruction, continues the tradition of beliefs and order of past generations, information that is only valuable if applied with respect to the culture of the present.

What has all this to do with the architecture of schools? The answer is a lot, but not enough. In the sixties and seventies, we had the opportunity to design private schools that provided public education (during the opposition to the Franco regime in Spain). We had time to discuss with teachers and pedagogues how they would like to teach different ages and how different subjects needed different strategies and tactics.

The importance of turning every space into an educational opportunity had to be allied to the importance of communication, teamwork, and social contacts between pupils and teachers from other classrooms. This emphasises the value of social spaces both inside and outside. We carried on these discussions over several years with different schools, and at the same time we investigated experiences in England, Holland, Denmark and Italy, visiting schools and government officials and also reading publications from the U.S.

The first school we designed was *Sant Gregori* for the city of Sabadell, near Barcelona, which simulated a cluster of homes around a public square (classrooms around a hall). This was never built. The second was *Garbi* in the Barcelona suburb of Esplugues de Llobregat to be built in two stages, first primary education, with classrooms around a large dining hall (respect for the importance of the social tradition of a formal Mediterranean meal), and then the second stage, for secondary education, conceived as a street leading away from the square.

The square itself was surrounded by wide "streets" on two levels, linking the homes (with fully glazed windows visually embracing the work areas of the "streets"). The pedagogy of Garbi followed straight from its origins in the *Escola del Mar* on the Barcelona beach in the thirties.

Our third school was *Costa i Llobera*, on the hillside above Barcelona. Because of its in-house, non-religious and experimental educational programme this one had difficulties with the political regime. The fourth was Thau, an all-age, mixed, lay school promoted by active progressive Christians, built on the city's edge, touching the wealthier districts of Barcelona, where nearly all the new private schools were being built.

Again a compact plan with an interior, stepped, court which gave ventilation and light to the extensive "public" areas, including an open library and various top-lit science laboratories. Several of the features proposed for *Costa i Llobera* were incorporated. *Costa i Llobera* was built later, due to the political hostility from the city authorities. So ideas flowed from earlier schools, but the experience of *Thau* followed on to *Costa i Llobera* and others, including more public schools when a fragile democracy arrived in 1980.

All our architecture for schools reflects two major principles. The first is free education for all. This is emphasised in their close relationship to the street, rather than being lost in vast sports fields and so separated from their urban context. Secondly, continuing this idea of a close relationship to the street, is exploiting the opportunity of using the school for adult education and weekend use for the children. This aspect opens up the possibility of including the whole of the city, town and village as an educational space, a lifetime experience, each place with reference to its physical and cultural identity.

How the space is arranged to encourage team work between the pupils themselves and between them and the teacher is crucial. How the student occupies the space can be seen immediately by observing how the tables and chairs are distributed in the classroom and how much space there is for social contact and studies beyond the classroom. Both are important. The classroom arrangement determines the balance between education and instruction. If the corridor is just a narrow link it restricts opportunities. The wide vitality of a 'street' brings casual contacts, with the stimulus of information from others.

"Architecture", according to Henry Morris, a former school inspector around Cambridge, England in the thirties, "is the ordering of the whole of our visual environment, and in architecture, thus conceived, I include not only the architect, the engineer and the craftsman, but also the sculptor, the painter and the landscapist. One of the main functions of architecture in high civilisation has been to give significance to man's physical environment, either in terms of feeling

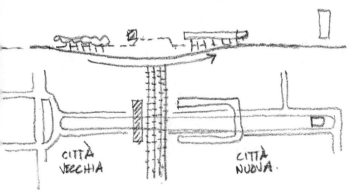

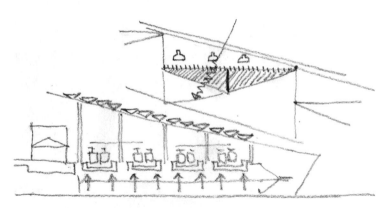

Urban design. Link under the railway station, Parma, Italy (2001)

Urban design. Railway station, Parma, Italy (2001)

Urban design. Bus station, Parma, Italy (2001)

Urban design. Sinking existing square, Parma, Italy (2001)

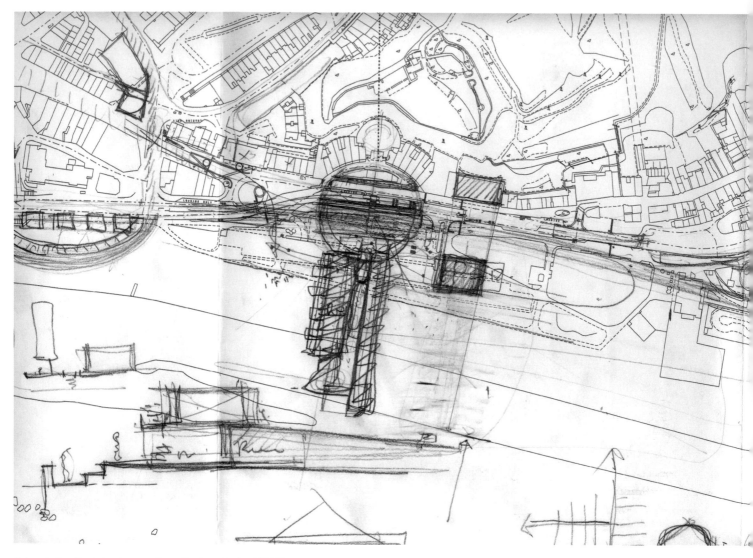

Urban design. Restoring the waterfront, Hastings, England (2002)

through awe and the numinous (the sense of what is hallowed and sacred) or in terms of the human body and its manifold states – all of these being human values of great importance and efficiency in the psychological, emotional, and physical life of man". (extract from a lecture in 1956).

I have selected relevant extracts from an interview with Joan Manuel del Pozo, doctor of philosophy, in 2008, entitled *The Beautiful Gives Knowledge and Goodness*. These ideas complement those of Henry Morris, and even remind me of William Morris, 150 years before.

Del Pozo opens the interview with ideas close to those of Herbert Read (1893-1968), the English poet and art critic, valuing art:

"The education of the beautiful is not a new idea or to vindicate that beauty in an educational context. In 1902, Adolphe Ferrière drew up 30 points for the New School and introduced the concept that the New School incorporates an atmosphere of beauty. This is a clear beginning in the field of pedagogy. On the other hand, I have found a remark of an elderly woman, modest, poor, and probably analphabetic from a "favela" in Brazil who said "we also have a right to beauty".

Extracting a patchwork of later concerns that seals the relation of art to education Del Pozo later remarks: "... we could say that a school is a place of beauty", and "precisely the beautiful is good for education because it builds up sensibility and invites respect", which leads him to add "the word respect gives us the key that relates aesthetics to ethics created through the sensation of balance, harmony, with blends and resonances that generate the capacity to capture the complexity of things".

A few years ago, I gave a lecture on the value of educational space to teachers at the annual "Rosa Sensat" Summer School in Barcelona. Afterwards many teachers complained to me that the more recent schools in Catalonia, under the younger national conservative government (CiU), had lost the emphasis on quality apparent in schools commissioned by the same party in the early days of post-Franco democracy. Classrooms were now just a string of boxes along a narrow corridor, losing the social spaces that allowed freer and unexpected communication between everyone.

School buildings were becoming dull and even depressing. Rules of design were standardised with little allowance to stimulate an emotional response, to encourage the imagination of both teachers and pupils. It was obvious that architects were too constrained to contribute to the aesthetic value of education The object of educational buildings had passed from future citizens to numbers. Aesthetic qualities were forgotten in the bowels of the financial department, due to the so-called debt crisis that governments are at a loss to explain. Confusion of thought adds to the confusion of language. Perhaps the schools or parents of some politicians were not up to the standard we imagined.

This response from the teachers was a sad commentary on a government that claims to be nationalist and patriotic. They lament a Catalonia that rightly has a proud history of eminent pedagogues and architects from the open air schools in the early decades of the 20th century to those in the dawn of a new democracy. A history that is still alive in the memory of many is that of Maria Montessori who was invited by the Barcelona City Council to visit the city and set up her teaching methods for schools. The city also began a series of schools by the eminent architect Josep Goday, whose designs provided an elegant classical environment for learning, *Baixeras* (1917-20), *Pere Vila* (1921), *Ramon Llull* (1921), *Milà i Fontanals* (1921), and not forgetting the *Escola del Mar* (1922).

The *Escola del Mar* was built on the beach of Barceloneta for children, frail in health, for whom the open air and sea provided a beneficial environment. The head teacher and pedagogue, Pere Vergés, adapted the 'New School' system that allowed the children to participate in many activities, the library, theatre and the ways of the weather and sea. The Escola del Mar was destroyed in the bombardment of 1938. The Garbi school (1962-68) was a "grandchild" of the Escola del Mar with Pere Vergés continuing as its first headmaster.

The open air school "Les Escoles del Bosc" in the Montjuic park (1910) and the Escola del Mar are two interesting examples that follow Jean-Jacques Rousseau's naturalist approach to education. They mixed boys and girls, allowing them to discover knowledge and respect contradictions and differences, in a free environment during their infant and early primary education.

Some European countries, like Germany and Austria, and exceptionally at Summerhill in England, run by the pedagogue A.S. Neill and his wife Ena, determined to make, "the school fit the child, instead of making the child fit the school". Considered extreme by some, these schools provided imaginative and self-confident people. Summerhill was later recognised by the educational authorities and by the United Nations.

Apart from the elegant classical schools in Barcelona, the rationalist phase of the Modern Movement also began to include interesting inside and outside spaces, like the courtyard classrooms by E. May in Frankfurt (1927), by J. Duiker in Amsterdam (1930) and by Terragni in Como (1936-37). This line of indoor and outdoor classrooms was continued after the Spanish Civil War by Martorell and Bohigas, with the school *El Timbaler del Bruc* (1957) by the Riera de Horta, a village incorporated near the edge of Barcelona.

This loosening up of the classroom space was more radical in England and California. The former eliminated the "room" for the "class" and exchanged them for various academic and pastoral areas, while the latter opted for just one simple space for all.

Given that a minority of teachers in Catalonia would be likely to digest these strong radical ideas within the current cultural tradition, we (MBM) compromised with linking every two classrooms for infants to suggest team teaching. We introduced a continuity of learning space to the common dining, acting, sleeping space with a "red line", established with three steps down from the classroom. This led us to imply that the spatial arrangement of the school should be considered as an urban space: the classrooms being the homes and the community spaces like streets and squares. It was a question of bringing the city into the school, which later led to bringing the school into the city.

Since most Catalans nowadays will either have been to one or more of these more open schools, or have accompanied their children, they will appreciate how important educational space is, in its dimensions, and how aesthetic quality influences the happy atmosphere. Some, of course, will have noticed its absence and how this difficulty is managed by imaginative teachers and directors.

The wealth and well-being of a nation lies in its people. If the nation does not put its people first, their education, research and imagination, then that nation is condemned to lose its freedom. One can observe, both in history and in the present, that education is the enemy of dictatorship. Dictatorship is afraid of knowledge, imagination and the diversity of ideas. They prefer mathematics, exact sciences and sport, which are seen to not challenge authority. The positive role of architecture is in the quality of space. When abandoned in favour of a militant obsession of repetition or a rigid discipline of systematic spaces, the environment is ignored.

Architecture forms the clothes of education, loose and colourful, warm or cool, free to allow spontaneous change or even discarded to allow the air and sun to cherish the body. Beauty, whatever its form, generates respect.

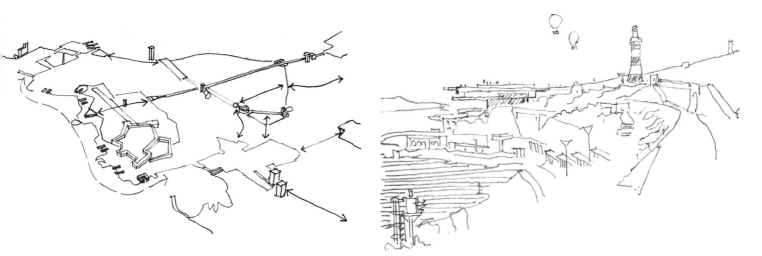

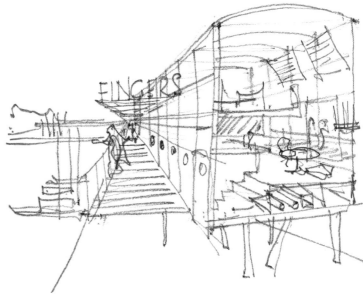

Urban design concept. Connecting. Plymouth, England (2003)

Urban design. Waterfront. The Hoe (sketchbook). Plymouth, England (2003)

Urban design. Half a bridge fish restaurant. Plymouth, England (2003)

Urban design. Finger lofts into old harbour. Plymouth, England (2003)

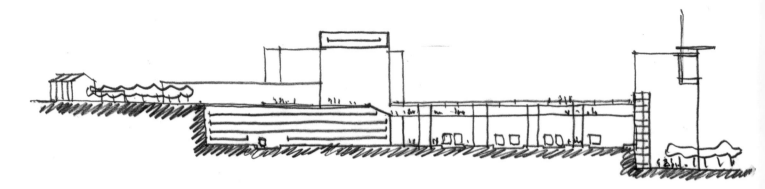

Urban design. Railway station hub. Plymouth, England (2003)

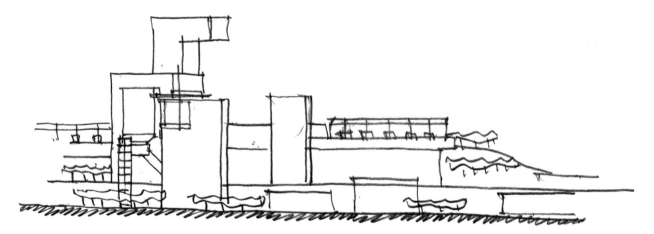

Urban design. Railway station hub. Plymouth, England (2003)

Urban design. Introducing housing in city centre. Plymouth, England (2003)

The Impending Disaster of Longer Living

If entering a discussion on education is a minefield, a discussion on old age is shrouded with wilful ignorance. That is until you find yourself there. Most people who consider "life expectancy" get the impression that, in the past, people died younger. We seem to be living longer as time goes by. The truth is that life expectancy has never changed by much for those who reach maturity. Life expectancy is calculated from birth.

Because in the past the medical support and medicines of today did not exist, early infant deaths, deaths of mothers in childbirth, illness, plagues and accidents all took their toll. Many died before the age of 15, then there were countless violent deaths in wars up to the age of 25. Those who were left survived normally to 50 or 70 years old. Life expectancy could only be calculated from the evidence of registers of birth and deaths. The change came when advanced medicine and proper medication became available for many at the beginning of the 20th century.

For example, in the classical Greek period the average life expectancy was 28 years but for those who reached 15, life expectancy was 52. In medieval Britain average life expectancy was 31 years. The 2010 average was 67 years. It is clear that improvements in medicine have brought about this general increase in longevity. This is a powerful argument for maintaining public health services of high quality for the whole population.

Healthcare is not alone in supporting a greatly increased life expectancy. Nutrition, living conditions, social networks and care, and the variables of population increase and decrease all affect how long we live. We hear dramatic references to a potential disaster of a very elderly population approaching rapidly, due to the fall in the birth-rate. There are predictions of greatly reduced economic support for the elderly and their care. This has now been aggravated by the greed of some institutions, causing financial markets to collapse, leading to unsustainable unemployment of over 50% of the young in some European nations, brutal effects on the middle aged, and the possible abandonment of the elderly. There is growing alarm about the increasing population below the poverty line.

There is a further question concerning the social isolation of elderly people that should be considered beyond even the risk of their confinement to home. That is the urban quality of the area where they live. In his *Life Between Buildings* (1980) Jan Gehl warned of lifeless cities and residential areas arising from de-industrialisation, the segregation of various city functions, and reliance on the automobile. All these factors have caused cities to become duller. These issues point up another important need, namely, the need for "social stimulation".

Gehl goes on to comment that "older people represent a particularly colourful and attractive opportunity for stimulation, and the negative fact that nothing happens because nothing happens".

Children would rather stay in and watch TV because it is dull outside. Older people do not find it entertaining to sit down on benches to watch the world go by, because there is almost nothing to see. When there are few children playing, few people sitting on benches, and few walking by, it is not very interesting to look out of windows, there is not much to see.

The need for social stimulation for the isolated elderly remains an important factor to be considered. It should not be excluded from the physical needs of the dwelling.

These comments on the isolation of low density suburbs of northern and mid-European cities and towns contrast with the constant movement in the open spaces between the high density of the Mediterranean South. High density however often means high buildings and more isolated dwellings above the top six floors.

Urban design within the old city, 's-Hertogenbosch, Netherlands (2003)

"All the lonely people", the Beatles' *Eleanor Rigby* lyric, magnificently illustrates the social isolation of big cities:

I look at all the lonely people
I look at all the lonely people
Eleanor Rigby picks up the rice in the church
Where a wedding has been
Lives in a dream
Waits at the window, weaving the face that she
Keeps in a jar by the door
What is it for?
All the lonely people
Where do they all come from?

Behind this lyric is the empathy between the young (the Beatles) and the elderly, their grandparents' generation. The common understanding between the young, who can also feel isolated and the elderly, has a social lesson in the design of dwellings and the design of cities with shared places, be they inside or outside, near or on ground level.

Another key question is when do we become elderly? Evidently every individual is different and accepts the circumstances differently, some as a liberation and some with resignation. Many people retire at, say 65, more or less and begin to receive a pension. Many others wish to continue working and some of the privileged, like doctors or architects, or actors and artists, do so and are not considered a burden on society. Local shopkeepers around the corner seem to go on forever, like their shops.

Longevity or a stable life was first challenged by Richard Sennet (a musician turned urban sociologist and writer) who observed that in the States "a job for life" had ended. If I remember right, he reckoned everyone was beginning to change their job perhaps twenty times in their lifetime, and

Urban design within the old city, 's-Hertogenbosch, Netherlands (2003)

even their profession three times. Mobility was now the way up, rather than stability. This also has had a negative effect on the family structure when both partners are working and changing school for children a problem. Life according to Sennet was beginning to get complicated. Separations increased and created the new social qualification of a single parent.

The house building industry, in Spain at least, has apparently ignored all these social changes, churning out three bedroom-plus homes for everyone. Advertising seems to suffer the same social ignorance. Some, including a few architects, are beginning to respond to the reality of social change, but we still have an enormous stock of old housing, either too big or too small for adapting and sharing.

There is no agreed date when you begin to feel elderly. You may wish to retire or you may be obliged to, but even that is not related to the personal reality of suddenly finding yourself

on the way. The reality just creeps up without you noticing, or rather perhaps you are determined not to notice it. Through habit you hold the necessary cash in hand to pay the adult entrance fee to an exhibition, or see a film. Being 'mistaken' for being elderly excites you with the possibility of paying less when you still feel young.

Following everyone else into the metro, or tube in London, there is a crush while everyone tries to find a place of support. Then, just when you have found a strap to hang on, a young woman takes pity on you, gets up and offers her seat to you, in front of the general public who, you are convinced, share her compassion. At that moment you have begun another life. There is no going back. But you will go on resisting, trying to keep up a sportingly youthful appearance to avoid another embarrassing situation.

Genetically women have no way out, the process of growing older starts when their ovulation packs up and they can no longer conceive. Men on the other hand struggle on as best as they can, thinking that, if Picasso or Charlie Chaplin could, why shouldn't they? The other event, over which you have no control, is the wonderful arrival of your first grandchild. That happened to me when I was only forty-eight.

On my way to the hospital to greet the happy couple I passed a day residence for what was called the "Third Age". Through the window there were a group of elderly men playing dominos and a separate group of elderly women chatting. No doubt they were what you might expect ultimately to be, normal grandparents. I had great respect for them but definitely did not wish to be classified in the "Third Age" with them, refusing my generational upgrading to attend a day centre so early.

Aging takes its own time for each person. We can generalise simply by observation of what happens to ourselves and to those around us. Sight, for example, has no regular timetable. People of all ages seem to need spectacles. It is only when we notice that we get more tired reading that we begin to have to adjust to new habits, like better light, or avoiding books with small print. Hearing is somewhat different as it implies difficulties with other people who begin to shout or get annoyed when you set the volume of the TV set too high. Loss of memory begins with taking time to remember. In a group of friends you share this problem and laugh when one of you finally remembers first.

The playwright, novelist and Queen's Counsel (a senior barrister or advocate), John Mortimer, in one of his autobiographies, describes that the first warning of restricted mobility is when you find your pale foot wandering through the air to find the opening of your sock. This is followed with stupid, humiliating and comical falls. He warns that "no one should grow old who is not ready to appear ridiculous". I mention all these circumstances of getting old. Myself, at eighty, I have begun to notice them all.

Before we can relate the elderly population to architecture, and all that it involves, we need to understand what it means to be elderly. On one hand, we must appreciate the value of experience to the community, and on the other hand, allow people to retain their independence.

To segregate an important part of this population into private residences, because of mobility or senility issues is understandable when the family cannot cope at home. However, given that 80% of the elderly wish to stay in their own home and neighbourhood then the solution is to take care of the carers. They need it, and it is likely to be more economical. This is one of the great challenges of our era. Architects, along with other professionals, can help to provide the solution.

Considering a methodology of architecture for the elderly the first move is to follow the example of Ildefons Cerdà. We must begin with a social survey of the housing conditions and location of where the elderly are living, neighbourhood by neighbourhood. Handfuls of architects, together with other professionals have already started pilot studies on their own in more than one urban settlement.

Younger professionals are finding a new social and professional role, to organise how to economically adapt dwellings and neighbourhoods that could remain home for the 80% of the elderly who wish to continue living there. This experience and information will allow municipal authorities to coordinate and evaluate a strategy to utilise the skills of local professionals in the building industry. For example to select appropriate streets, near to where elderly people are living, and to adapt the dwellings there to the essential necessities of the elderly.

Simple examples of appropriate adaptation would be taps and handles which are easy to turn, exchanging baths for showers, easy access and handles for WCs, safer kitchens, even armchairs that are easier to get up from and of course a suitable mobile phone for communication or to seek help. I understand that the city of Bristol has been able to undertake this on a budget of £1750 per dwelling, converting around fifteen dwellings at a time with a local builder and other professionals.

Some of the challenges facing the increasingly elderly population are, to quote "The Ageing Housing and Ageing Alliance", as follows:

First, the big issues for health:

- many of the most chronic health conditions (heart disease, stroke, respiratory conditions, arthritis) have causal links to housing conditions, and
- almost two thirds of general and acute hospital beds are occupied by people over 65.

A brief reflection on costs:

- £ 35,100 pays for one nursing home place,
- £ 35,000 provides 200 older people with minor household adaptions,
- £ 1 billion, the annual cost of falls amongst older people in the UK,
- £ 30,000, the cost of one hip fracture,
- £ 4,000, the cost of extra home care of a year's delay in home adaptations.

Second, the big issue for housing and planning:

- nearly a third of all homes are already lived in by people over retirement age, and
- older people will account for nearly half of new household growth in 2026.

Although this may read like a government white paper, it does give food for thought, implying that very significant monies can be saved if a minor amount is invested with a few simple adaptations to the existing housing stock.

For some time I have thought that for children we have education that prepares them for adult life. For the employed

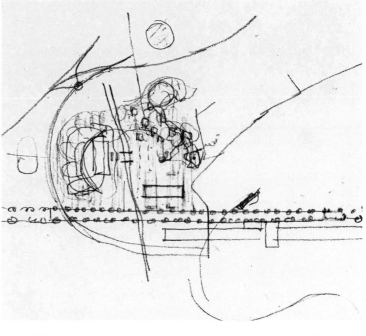

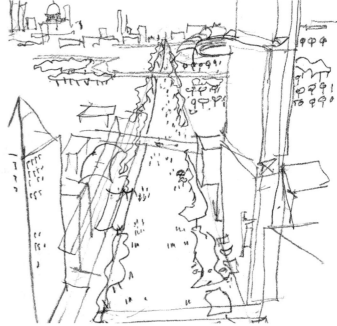

London Olympics urban design, Lea Valley, London, England (2006)

we have the trade unions and legislation. There is little, if any, education during middle age to prepare for being elderly. There is no union to support the rights and opportunities of the elderly or for that matter the neglected unemployed.

There are many cases of ill-treatment of the elderly. These include shifting them off to residences, away from normal life and contact with other generations. Western culture has not adjusted to the loss of the historic, three generation, family unit. The breakdown began with the shift from rural environments to industrial towns, though street communities did substitute for the village for quite a while.

In between these reflections I also have a personal gripe about how unprotected older people seem to be from the exploitation of package holidays. Many of us have seen, or even been involved in, groups of middle-aged and elderly people, converged like cattle on cheap flights, coaches, and in canteen hotels around the world. The elderly are worth more than this.

The majority I am sure would like more active ageing. They have a great deal of generous wisdom to help business and the creative industries, even if only to contribute a few hours sharing experience and imagination. They could swing the balance in education for the young, assist the work of the middle-aged, keep a weather eye against corruption, and help to make elections more democratic. Older people can also encourage others to be more tolerant of different cultures and changing values, and last, but not least, keep an eye on the repair and care of their city, town or village.

If people retire around fifty or sixty, they have another twenty-five or more years to contribute to the welfare of their fellow citizens. There are going to be a lot of elderly around to help and be helped. It is time that our elected political representatives woke up to this huge issue.

So how can architecture help the elderly? Sue Adams, now chief executive of "Care and Repair UK", is very clear on what needs to be done. It needs an interaction between

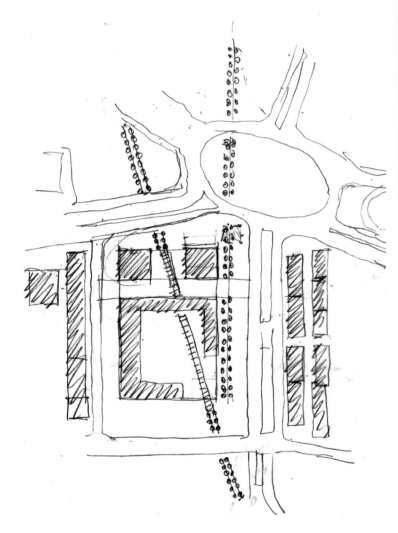

Tecnocampus University urban design, Mataró, Barcelona, Catalonia (2006)

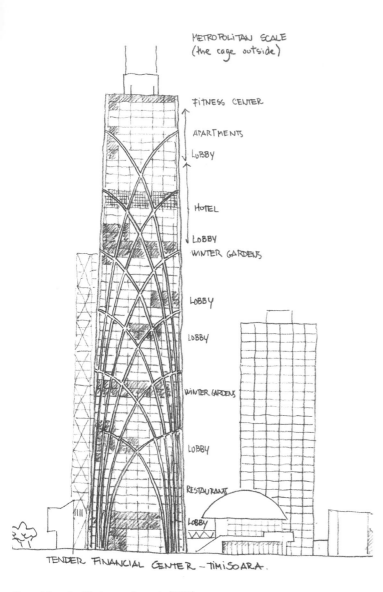

METROPOLITAN SCALE
(the cage outside)

FITNESS CENTER

APARTMENTS

LOBBY

HOTEL

LOBBY
WINTER GARDENS

LOBBY

LOBBY

WINTER GARDENS

LOBBY

RESTAURANT

LOBBY

TENDER FINANCIAL CENTER - TIMISOARA.

Financial centre, Timisoara, Romania (2013)

health, social-care and housing. They form a triangle, like a three legged stool, if you are missing one angle or leg, it is unbalanced. That is what is happening today, as housing and the built environment are generally missing.

Functionally obsolete buildings within a neighbourhood can also offer accommodation for the elderly while adaptions are being carried out to their homes nearby, ensuring that they do not leave familiar territory and their own neighbours.

Architects should also spot opportunities where new designs are needed. Now is the time to consider the needs of the elderly. It is good to remember that the affluent also grow old and can afford to adapt their own dwellings. They can help through prompting the creation of new designs that may, in time, be available to all. One example lies in the field of wheelchairs. Although practical, they can be difficult to accept, sadly tainted with social stigma. Just think a Formula One wheelchair would be the envy of the neighbourhood.

We should also remember that education never stops. A pleasant environment, both inside and out, contributes to the wellbeing of the elderly as well. Beauty should always be present, a simple bunch of flowers, arranged by someone with skill and an eye, can be magical.

"The best time of our life is when we are elderly", said Sibyl Moholy-Nagy, the professor of Architectural History at Pratt Institute, NY the day after Christmas when I met her in Barcelona. She was well into her old age and added "you have nothing to lose, and people are generally polite and listen to you". Wisdom assembled through years of critical repetition is often good advice, especially when accompanied with a modest dose of doubt.

With a few technical refinements and a thoughtful rearrangement of the space, architecture can help the elderly to go on living in their own homes. Calm and contented they can look out of the window they have always looked out of at the neighbourhood and the friends they have always known.

I have no idea when I drew the little group protesting, or for
what. At this moment I believe it is time that everyone should
understand the cultural value of architecture in helping us
all to recognise that beauty counts before avarice.

EPILOGUE:
The City: a Landscape Strewn with Political Ignorance

In Shakespeare's *As You Like It* Jaques stands apart from life with his monologue upon the Seven Ages of Man. His metaphor has supplied the structural stream of this book on architecture to give the proverbial "man in the street" a better understanding of the street itself and, incidentally, his or her own home.

The idea that "All the world's a stage and all the men and women merely players" is a notion that everyone has entertained in one moment or other, looking out of the window or sitting on a bench watching the world go by. We observe the actors but forget that the seven ages of man brings home to us the cruel reality that our own lives are like a drop of water in the ocean of time. This must surely increase our respect for the built heritage around us. However, it also has another reading in that the city must be a stage for actors of all ages.

Shakespeare's characters, in their diversity and contradictions, reflect the liberty and restrictions of urban and rural life. In the case of this play the urban citizens seek to find the romance they imagine within the rural idyll of the Forest of Arden. At the end of the day the forest tires them and they long to return to the city. He could as well have set the scene the other way around, with the country folk going up to town for a day, or night, to seek a different stage to play out their desire of freedom.

The point of this book has been to examine the attractions of the urban stage –its architecture that embraces us through our lifetime, both for those that live there and those that only come for a visit. Apart from the urban stage there is also the rural stage for those who venture from the city to the countryside with its villages and country houses, half hidden in the landscape of water, crag and green. That however is another story.

Today everyone's window is his camera or mobile phone. These frozen images, or brief videos, only touch the scene for a moment. Our streets and the buildings that frame them, offer much more to the imagination, allowing us to interpret our own observations. Architectures are the clothes that enclose our space, and at the same time demonstrate to others who we are. Each building contains its own history, each street its own character, each city its geography and everywhere are the footprints of past generations. Each building is a unique part of the city.

Some buildings are good and beautiful, the fruit of long thought and hard work. Some are shoddy and badly dressed, made by the lazy minds of those ignorant of the wellbeing which architecture contributes to society or worse driven only by avaricious objectives. Oddly enough a city would not be real if it did not include the ugly building now and again (and future architects would not have enough to do!). Architecture reflects to the cultural pulse of citizens, and the city is valued for its diversity.

The architecture of a city begins with its streets. It draws its identity from its buildings. Streets belong to the people who live or work there, but they also connect and allow movement. That movement must be punctuated with a square or important building to guide people through the images of memory. Cities must be cared for, and now and again, repaired. They should never be destroyed, because they belong to their citizens. The city is their home, their place of work and where they enjoy moments among families and friends, forming the community.

Those who neglect who they are meant to represent when elected, and those who are lazy public servants of the people who pay them, threaten to damage or even destroy the city. These politicians run the risk of sleeping on a volcano that will undermine political legitimacy that in the long run will establish a fertile ground for political upheaval. Such a drama is already unfolding within a landscape strewn with political ignorance in London, Madrid and Barcelona, great cities and countries that are not alone.

A spontaneous revolt caused the Bastille to fall in 1789 and prepared the ground for the proclamation of the Republic in 1792. Like the October Revolution in 1917, the French over a century before opened the way for a new social and political era. However high hopes are often betrayed in these delicate situations.

Small events and the persistent oppression of the weakest can lead to catastrophe. The consistent undermining of the human foundations of a sound economy, together with a war against culture –the nerve centre of imaginative intelligence and education of future generations- make it difficult to believe declarations from political parties, clinging to power.

The bubble in the building industry is partly to blame for financial corruption and the bank crisis. The investment banks took over large construction firms. On the philosophy of the phrase "safe as houses", people were led to believe this was the best place for investment. The speed of internet financial deals made it difficult to control. Wealthy elderly bankers got strangely richer, no questions asked. All this was happening, not against the law. It was the land of the wild west, where law did not exist.

Rogue construction companies hit gold. Governments and civil servants became involved and kept quiet as long as everyone was happy spending on their plastic cards. In Spain an ignorant Government changed the laws to allow building anywhere, convinced that this would bring land values and building costs down. They went up. The architects' professional bodies warned Aznar's government of the danger but that fell on deaf ears.

Architects were, and are too often still, considered as expensive decorators. They are likely to be eliminated from commissions which are going to the very large umbrella organisations. In 2011 the Royal Incorporation of Architects in Scotland produced a report on public procurement called *Building a Better Future?* This has helped persuade the Scottish Government of the economic advantages of good design, opening a channel to revive public investment, badly needed for the economy. Perhaps this report can David-like throw a stone to overcome a catastrophic situation. Intelligent ideas, well written, can go a long way.

The Modern Movement in architecture was born with the Renaissance and has adapted to the contemporary reality of the citizen as the real client. It has evolved through wars and revolutions and will no doubt stand by its social and human responsibilities, emerging from the arid landscape that surrounds too many of us today.

BIBLIOGRAPHY AND REFERENCES

A Short Introduction

- *The Complete Works of William Shakespeare*, edited by Allen Lane, The Penguin Press. 1969, *As You Like It*, Introduction by Ralph Sergent.
- *History of Art in Antiquity*, Perrot and Chiprez, Chapman and Hall, 1883.
- *Architecture*, W.R. Lethaby, The Home University Library, revised 1939, Thorton Butterworth Ltd.
- *The Architecture of Humanism*, Geoffrey Scott, The Architectural Press, 1980 (original edition 1914).
- *The Architecture of Space*, Bruno Zevi, Horizontal Press N.Y, 1957.
- *Renzo Piano*, Massimo Dini, Electa/Architectural Press, N.Y, 1983.
  A phrase attributed to R.P, often cited in a similar language.
- *How to play the Chess Openings*, Eugene A. Znosko-Borovsky, Frank Hollings. 1935.

All the World's a Stage

- *The Opening Game*, Ludek Pachman, Routledge and Kegan Paul, 1982.
  (The actual game between Karpov and Korchnoi in March 1974 can be found in chapter 6 page 95: 1e4-c5, Nt3-d6 etc.)

- *A Life in Cities*, an Architectural Autobiography, David Mackay, Royal Incorporation of Architects in Scotland, 2009.
- Museo de la Vida Rural, Espluga de Francolí, restored and extended by the architect Dani Freixas and his team. 2009. See catalogue *La força de la mà de l'home*, available from the museum.
- *Cities, Corners*, Manuel de Solà-Morales, Catalogue, Forum Barcelona, 2004
- *Corridors of Power*, C.P. Snow, MacMillan, Penguin Books, 1966-1972.
- *The Holy State and the Profane State*, Thomas Fuller, 1642. The Concise Oxford Dictionary of Quotations, 1981.
- *Florence and Baghdad: Renaissance Art and Arab Science* by Hans Belting, review by Julian Bell in the London Review of Books, 25th October 2012.
- *Walt Whitman, the Complete Poems*, Penguin Books ed. 1979. Leaves of Grass: "Give me the Splendid Silent Sun" page 337.

And All the Men and Women Merely Players

- *"There is no such thing as society"*, Prime Minister Margaret Thatcher talking to *Women's Own* Magazine, October 31st 1987.
- *Cities in Evolution*, Patrick Geddes, William and Norgate, 1913.

- *Cities and People*, Mark Girouard, Yale University Press, 1985. (The quotation from Raymond Chandler is from one of his crime novels, page 255. Mark Girouard's book flows lightly, but thoroughly, through the history of cities all over the world and can be recommended for further reading).
- *William Morris*, Philip Henderson, Pelican Biographies, 1973. (Quotation from the lecture *The Lesser Arts*, 1877 related functional simplicity in *The Art of Life*, published in *Hopes and Fears of Art*, Illis and White, 1882. See also the magnificent biography *William Morris, a Life for Our Time*, Fiona McCarthy, Faber and Faber, 1994).
- *Hard Times*, Charles Dickens, Chapman and Hall and Henry Frowde within the Fireside edition, c. 1900. (The quotation can be found in chapter 10).
- *Cities for People*, Jan Gehl, Island Press, 2010.
- *The Corrosion of Character*, Richard Sennett, Norton and Company, N.Y., London. 1998.
- *The Summer of a Dormouse*, John Mortimer, Viking Penguin Books, 2000.

Published books

- *Contradictions in Living Environment*, London, Crosby Lockwood and Son Ltd, 1971. Spanish edition: *Contradicciones en el Entorno Habitado*, Barcelona, Gustavo Gili, 1972
- *Wohnungsbau im Wandel, Stuttgart*, Gerd Hatje, 1977. English edition: *Multiple Family Housing*, New York, Architectural Book Publishing Co., 1977. Spanish edition: *Viviendas Plurifamiliares*, Barcelona, Gustavo Gili, 1979
- *La Casa Unifamiliar, The Modern House*, Barcelona, Gustavo Gili, 1984. English edition: *The Modern House*, New York, Hastings House Publishers Inc., 1984. German edition: *Einfamilienhäuser*, Stuttgart, Gerd Hatje, 1984
- *Modern Architecture in Barcelona (1854-1939)*, Sheffield, The Anglo Catalan Society, 1985. Catalan edition: *L'Arquitectura Moderna a Barcelona (1854-1939)*, Barcelona, Edicions 62, 1989. English edition: *Modern Architecture in Barcelona (1854-1939)*, Oxford, BPS Professional Books, 1989. Berlín, Ernst und Sohn, 1989. New York, Rizzoli, 1989
- *La Recuperació del Front Marítim, Model Barcelona, Quaderns de gestió*, Barcelona, Aula Barcelona, Fundació Bosch i Gimpera i Universitat de Barcelona, gener de 2000
- David Mackay, Roger Zogolvitch, Martin Harradine. *A vision for Plymouth*, University of Plymouth, Plymouth, 2004
- *Català de Retruc*, Edicions de 1984, Barcelona, 2005
- *A Life in Cities, An Architectural Autobiography*, The Royal Incorporation of Architects in Scotland, Edinburgh, 2009

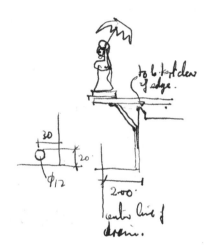

to b kept clear
of edge.

30

20

φ12

2·00

centre line of
drain.